THE NINE MODERN DAY MUSES (AND A BODYGUARD)

10 Guides to Creative Inspiration
for Artists, Writers, Lovers,
and Other Mortals Wanting to Live
a Dazzling Existence

By Jill Badonsky

Copyright © Jill Baldwin Badonsky, 2024
All rights reserved

Grateful acknowledgment is made for permission to reprint the following:

An excerpt from STAND STILL LIKE THE HUMMINGBIRD, copyright © 1962 by Henry Miller. Reprinted by permission of New Directions Publishing Corp.

An excerpt from A RETURN TO LOVE by Marianne Williamson, copyright © 1992 by Marianne Williamson. Reprinted by permission of HarperCollins Publishers Inc.

JUST DO IT™ is a registered trademark of Nike

LIBRARY OF CONGRESS CATALOGING-IN-PUBLICATION DATA
Badonsky, Jill Baldwin.
The nine modern day muses (and a bodyguard) : 10 guides to creative inspiration for artists, writers, lovers, and other mortals wanting to live a dazzling existence / Jill Baldwin Badonsky.
p. cm.

ISBN 979-8-218-36288-1

1. Creative ability. 2. Self-actualization (Psychology). I. Title.

Without limiting the rights under copyright reserved above, no part of this publication may be reproduced, stored in or introduced into a retrieval system, or transmitted, in any form, or by any means (electronic, mechanical, photocopying, recording, or otherwise), without the prior written permission of both the copyright owner and the above publisher of this book.

The scanning, uploading, and distribution of this book via the Internet or via any other means without the permission of the publisher is illegal and punishable by law. Please purchase only authorized electronic editions, and do not participate in or encourage electronic piracy of copyrighted materials. Your support of the author's rights is appreciated.

This book is printed on acid-free paper.

Dedicated to
My Mom
My very first Muse

"I am my own muse.
I am the subject I know best.
The subject I want to know better."
~Frida Kahlo

You are your own muse.

"Never forget that the nurturing and preservation
of your own muse is job one.
Lose it and you may be losing a great deal."
~Robert Genn

This book will help you nurture and preserve your own muse.

Contents:

Preface 8

PART ONE
Stuff in the Front 13

The Emergence of the Modern Day Muses 14

Welcome to the Mystery 17

The Mystery of Creativity 18

Entering the Garden of the Illustrious Muses 20

Equipment Needed for the Journey 24

A Muse Primer 25

AHA-PHRODITE:
Muse of Paying Attention, Passion, and Possibilities 37

ALBERT:
Muse of Imagination and Innovation 45

BEA SILLY:
Muse of Play, Laughter, and Dance 61

MUSE SONG:
Muse of Nurturing, Encouragement, and Good Company 77

SPILLS:
Muse of Practice, Process and Imperfection 89

AUDACITY:
Muse of Courage and Uninhibited Uniqueness 105

LULL:
Muse of Pause, Diversion, and Gratitude 119

SHADOW:
Muse of the Dark Side 130

MARGE:
Muse of Okay-Now-Let's-Get-Started 137

Name Yourself and Your Powers 150

Creativity is a
life driven
by courage.

Preface

ANOTHER FINE MYTH

On a warm, still day in the reverie of a café near the ocean, I sat sipping a latte as the bougainvillea felt inspired to throw purple petals on my writing notebook. I was recuperating from a job chosen by my fears, not my heart. Once again, I had ignored my creative passions due to something silly ... like security.

Recently, I had started paying attention to my odd reactions to the jobs that led me away from the genuine creative expression I believe I was meant to share during my stay on the planet. When I take a job simply for financial security and disregard the skills that bring me joy—writing, teaching, art, or performance—I basically become a complete moron. I become incapable of anything but a series of blunders. It is as if I intentionally sabotage myself so that I can't work in such situations. I think this is the message: I'M NOT SUPPOSED TO BE IN SUCH SITUATIONS. I'm supposed to be truer to who I am.

My last job took me so far off my path of creative expression that the spell of stupidity I fell under made the need for public flogging the only acceptable outcome I was creating. I was constantly losing little things—like entire mailing lists, keys, and paychecks. I would regularly trip over furniture, computer equipment, and the occasional client. My shoulder pads would end up on the outside of my dress by the day's end (it was the early 90s so, yeah, shoulder pads)... a sure sign one is in the wrong place. Obviously, I was not really there ... mentally, spiritually or effectively. I was a blockhead masquerading so as to fit into a round slot.

Reaching my threshold of humiliation, I finally took the leap out of the job, without any support waiting for me (at least in the form that I had been accustomed to), and looked up into the fluff of the clouds and asked, "HELLO? ...JUST WHAT IS IT THAT I'M SUPPOSED TO DO?... I KNOW IT HAS SOMETHING TO DO WITH CREATIVITY, BUT COULD YOU GET A LITTLE MORE SPECIFIC?" I could use a miracle at that point. I knew what was next had to be something creative because my soul was pestering me regularly to release my inner creative-related rumbles. What I soon found out was that all sorts of people seem to be experiencing just about the same thing. Maybe you're one of them.

While musing about what truly motivated me, I realized I was obsessed with the creative process and had applied this obsession to writing and performing plays, writing columns, telling stories with multimedia, painting mixed media, drawing cartoons, joining an improvisational comedy troupe, public speaking in unpredictably irreverent ways. I was deepening my passion for teaching and coaching people on how to find and follow their creative passion mainly because I believed it could be done in a way that inspires people despite their human tendencies. "I think it's time to write a book," I thought. "If only I could get over the resistance to starting, the fear that it will be no good, the possibility that there are already enough books on the subject, the responsibility it implies, and the feeling that I do not know what I am doing (i.e., if only I could use what I am teaching)."

I looked up from my latte's snowy foam to see nine Muses sidling up to my table with expressions of suppressed laughter, and the kind of raised eyebrows that foretell impending surprise. These Muses, however, were not of ancient Greece. They were a new and improved, updated variety— colorful, hip, full of chutzpah—and they had a Bodyguard with them. They pulled chairs up to my table and stared directly into my bewilderment.

Well, eight of them did. One of them refused to sit because she was attaching a candy dispenser to a beanie cap.

Another one, who introduced herself as Aha-phrodite, seemed to be the spokes-muse. She informed me that it was time for the mortal public to learn about the Modern Day Muses. "It is especially important now," she explained, "when so many mortals are unfulfilled because they have abandoned the expression of their creative gifts and inclinations and gotten stuck into places of unfulfilling routine." So, a more relevant and savvy breed of Muses was now required to meet the challenge of inspiring ideas, follow- through, and fulfillment for these misguided modern mortals. And here they were ... in all their glory, at my table in the sun.

They introduced themselves one at a time: Aha-phrodite, Muse of Paying Attention and Possibilities; Albert, Muse of Imagination and New Thinking; Bea Silly, Muse of Childlike Play; Spills the Imp, Muse of

Practice, Process, and Imperfection; Audacity, Muse of Courage and Uninhibited Uniqueness; Lull, Muse of Pause, Diversion, and Gratitude; Shadow, Muse of the Gifts of the Dark Side; Muse Song, Muse of Encouragement, Nurturing, and Good Company; Marge, Muse of Okay-Now-Let's-Just-Get-Started; and the Bodyguard, who protects us from blocks, fears, and abandonment. (I called the Bodyguard, Arnold in the first and second issue, but now you get to conjure up your own bodyguard image).

I admit, I was bemused by their presence and a little afraid they would want me to buy them all coffee and bagels. Existing on savings and newly developing freelance work, (the allure of working for someone else was beyond resuscitation), I was a bit prudent with expenditures. Marge, the Muse of Okay-Now-Let's-Just-Get-Started, assured me that, yes, you betcha, they did want coffee, but to worry about income when an experience of such flow and fascination was about to be unveiled was just plain silly. The Muses were here to inspire a book that would not only introduce them to the masses of individuals interested in giving voice to the soul's creative authenticity, but would also provide practical exercises to make these concepts absorbable and effective. So I bought them all double mocha cappuccinos and a variety of scones. Except for Bea Silly—she wanted a cupcake with a small rotating flowerpot on top. Do they make those yet?

...

The Reality

All nine new Muses were there ... in the spirit of my imagination. I started toying with the idea of turning creative concepts into personas of Muses just for the fun of it, or perhaps because I was spending too much time alone. Anyway, I told a friend, Jennifer, about the Muses. She was in the middle of creating a business and was tickled by how my Muses could help her. Coming up against an obstacle or a stumbling block, she would call me up and ask me which Muse could help:

"Who will help me create a clever price sheet to display my services?" I told her about Albert, he's all about thinking differently. "Who will get me to a place where I don't fear what people think when I make public presentations?" Audacity fit the bill with an infusion of courage. "Who will help focus me when I seem to do everything except the thing I'm supposed to do?" That would be Marge. "I'm not enjoying doing my work right now." Bea Silly and Lull then helped her out. "How do I deal with these voices inside my head that are ridiculing me and trying to sabotage everything I'm doing?" Muse Song would soothe the savage voices, and the Bodyguard would defend and reinforce her moves forward.

Jennifer would call me back enthusiastic from success, talking about the Muses as if I had dispatched them to her home like doctors making house calls. The Muses, of course, were only concepts to ignite her own strengths. They just made it clear what energy she could draw upon from *inside herself*. And pretending that they were actual entities made it fun and enticing then leads to motivation. Fun and play are what we engage in as children to lure us to the experiences that successfully serve us as adults. Hello! Let's get wise and use fun as adults to make the validating human experience of creativity more accessible.

Creativity gives us the optimal experience of what Mihaly Csikszentimihalyi has described as a state in which creative energy flows freely and effortlessly. He writes, "The process of discovery involved in creating something new appears to be one of the most enjoyable activities any human can be involved in." He explains that creativity is a central source of meaning in our lives. We bring something new, needed, or novel into existence and experience in the process a timeless flowing, a release from stress and of peak experiences.

Abraham Maslow describes self-actualization as a person's need to be, and do, that which the person was "born to do." When we feel something missing in our life, many times it is because we are not expressing that which we were born to share.

My mission in life is to deepen my own creativity and teach others to do the same. It's a passion. I'd do it for free if I could live off of oxygen alone.

If there is something that can make creativity fun and easier, hey, I'm for it! The Muses tell me this book will help.

The Nine
Modern Day Muses
(and a Bodyguard)

PART ONE
STUFF IN THE FRONT

The Emergence of the Modern Day Muses

Artist (n.)—Someone who chooses to share a creative call through the expression of artistic passions, the selection of thoughts that create joy, and the activation of authentic approaches to living life.
Someone who is not afraid to be his,
her, or their true self with others.
~Muse-kipedia

French Riviera, two in the afternoon. The nine Greek Muses, once beacons of creative inspiration, were lolling in the sun getting fat from pear tarts and chocolate éclairs. They sipped on the concoction of champagne and Tang they had invented that morning.

They invent things like that almost every day. They are, after all, a creative bunch, so why not? They are the Muses. The mythical girls from ancient Greece with the ability to inspire song, art, verse, and ... spanakopita. They give the i's dots. Yes, the i's of every i-dea . . . they provide inspiration, intuition, innovation, ingenuity, intrigue, interesting, invaluable qualities of waxing authentic, extraordinary, and other applicable i words that I may have forgotten like . . . maybe: incredible. They tango with the peculiar, dangle with participles, and dare mortals to "climb every mountain and follow every star," to "carry moonbeams home in a jar."

Those Muses ...

They were in the middle of an extended sabbatical on the French Riviera, a rest place away from the think-tank towers of Mount Olympus.

Okay, to tell you the truth, they were laid off in the Mount Olympus downsizing that happened May of last year. A survey taken by Hercules indicated that demand for their services had been in a critical decline since the invention of TV, the advent of the Internet, swerving intentions, deliberate avoidance, denial, denial of denial, immobilized good intentions, frozen interventions, abandoned renovations, incessant cleaning of kitchen counters, and a hypnotic trance toward the never-ending scroll of social media. And, to top it all off, modern mortals want things to be quick and easy. Creativity is a divine feature of ever new joy, but it simply cannot be categorized as "quick and easy."

The Muses were getting tired of the French Riviera and were ready to get back to what they loved the best: Inspiring mortals to make beautiful things and think thoughts that made life easier.

The heck with the layoff—being the resourceful beings they were, the Muses knew they could get their posts back. They know the power of trust over fear, and the difference between taking a break and complacency. They were just relishing the light in Provence. But things would have to be different.

They discussed their reemergence over papaya smoothies. And as their conversation progressed, the Muses became a little unsettled. Many mortals were not even listening. They were giving weak excuses about why they were not engaging in the spirited acts of creativity.

Yet the Muses were unfettered, mostly because they loved the word, "unfettered." The Muses love nothing better than to solve an unsettling, perplexing, and fetter-prone problem. And this was a big one.

They began by reviewing the facts. You see, every mortal is given the ability to dance with Creative Expression. Every mortal. Every, every, every mortal, even the ones who say, "Who me? ... Oh, no, no ... I'm not creative in the least bit." EVERYONE IS CREATIVE. The thoughts we think create the feelings we feel which create the actions we take. We have a choice. The palette of thoughts is filled with a gigantic selection of perspectives, attitudes, and angles. We create lists, plans, gardens, events, children, drama, healing. We create strategies, conspiracies, responses, vacations, solutions, and sauces for asparagus.

Every mortal has some way to be a creative beacon. Whether it be to make luscious variations of portobello spaghetti sauce, to write a ditty about falling stars for the girl at the wi-fi cafe, to invent a fugue in D, a duet in E, and a ballad in Biloxi, to dance wild new steps to silly old songs, to smile radiantly from the heart, or to create awe in the studio audience of the mind, of life, of the effervescent magic of the soul—every mortal has a creative light just waiting to shine brighter.

To be creative is, yes, to do art. It has also been identified as one of the top qualities of an effective manager and the edge a successful entrepreneur has on competitors. It is an inner beauty that radiates on the outside no matter what age you are. Creative expression is the beacon your soul mate will detect to find you. It is the key to relationships that flourish, and the means through which parenting becomes joyous. It is the tool that takes a mundane reality and makes it extraordinary. Creative problem solving is the answer to life's most challenging dilemmas. If you choose to be creative, life is a fulfilling journey where wonder awaits every twist of thought and turn of attitude.

All mortals have at their fingertips the great joy that comes from the delight in what they create. They have the colossal kick of a time-defying flow of present-moment bliss, the kind that comes when they engage ... in creating.

But they watch the blue screens of technology instead. So ...

Those Muses came up with a variety of ideas to redirect mortals. Their favorite was to reinvent themselves as Modern Day Muse Equivalents. They would become updated, savvy Muses, geared to combat the modern mortals' hard-core avoidance strategies. They would drop their old names, domains, and invent new ones. As they mused at their moxie, the Muses contemplated the big human truth:

> MORTALS MUST DO WHAT THEY ARE HERE TO CREATIVELY DO OR THEY WILL BECOME CRANKY.

The Muses decided this makeover would have to happen in order to stamp out irritability and lost potential. Therefore, they did reinvent themselves.

Now, they are eager to reveal the newly concocted modern secrets of creative inspiration.

My name is Jill. I channel Muses. For the last eleven years I have faithfully tuned in to the six o'clock Muse report bandwidth and frequency line. I have frantically taken down the daily Muse flashes. I have condensed the best parts into this book so I can share with you all the "Muse fit to print". There was a lot of undecipherable chatter, hysterical laughter, and mumbled musings that I didn't include, but I have notes if you want to see them.

So, let's begin. Let's excavate our dreams.

Sarah Ban Breathnach, author of *Simple Abundance*, says, "If we're unsure of our passions, we must continue excavating until we rediscover them, for if we don't find outward expression to our passions in little ways every day, we will eventually experience the spontaneous combustion of our souls."

And this can be very, very messy. I wouldn't know where to start cleaning up a combusted soul, would you?

Welcome to the Mystery

The Muses announced that in their new, updated, modern forms they would be hanging out in a metaphor. Since they are somewhat metaphorical themselves, we shouldn't be expecting to see them at Starbucks or Denny's. They chose the metaphor of a garden, specifically, the Amazing Garden of the Illustrious Muses. (Obviously, they feel very good about themselves - something mortals could learn from for creative success.) Come on in!

To get into a metaphor you must open your mind a bit and don a childlike awareness with a twist of imagination. Walk down your garden's path in a spirit of exploration and wonder. Pay attention to the experience beyond the intellect—the one within your intuition.

Intuition will amplify your courage, as Joseph Campbell says, "to leave behind the life you planned, in order to find the life that is awaiting you."

As you commit to taking small, low-pressured steps down the garden's path, a momentum will form that can lift you beyond your limitations. You may feel a charge of enthusiasm, compassion, and curiosity that comes with entering the realm of a mysterious process. What would it feel like to simply trust that beyond the painting, the poem, or the music you create, you are also creating a process of loving life more?

THE MYSTERY OF CREATIVITY

Creativity is a puzzle and a paradox. Artists, writers, scientists, rarely know how their original ideas arise so there may never be a scientific theory of creativity. The apparent unpredictability of creativity defies any scientific explanation or prescribed formula. Divine inspiration? Romantic intuition? Innovative insight? Indigestion?

The Muses explain that Ideas arise beyond the intellect, through intuition's flirtation with the subconscious. The more that we can trust ourselves, the freer our creativity is.

First we must give ourselves permission to go beyond our fears. Some of us miss out on a life of creative joy because we blindly listen to our fears and live a life based on their illusions. We fear inadequacy, we fear we will lose people or gain responsibility. We fear giving up comfortable routines, wasting time and resources, looking foolish. Money worries prevent us from pursuing that which does not ensure an income. We fear giving up a lifestyle filled with material objects for a life filled with creative expression, authenticity, and pure joy. Starting the creative process is hard work with no guarantees that we will succeed in the classic sense of financial success or artistic masterpieces.

How come such a process of joy brings up so many fears? The answer could be because creativity is the ultimate growth process; fear can be simply an affirmation that growth is happening. When we are unattached to the results of our creative journey, we can move through the fear and find rewards greater than the purpose that initially drew us to the journey. We may think we want to write a book or act or sing, but what we find if we stay on the path is a deeper experience of how to live life and love ourselves. The skills we obtain by saying yes to the creative process are skills we can use in all areas of our lives: flexibility, intuition, risk-taking, confidence, playfulness, open-mindedness, resourcefulness, acceptance, to name only a few. But these skills will only come with patience, willingness, and participation in the process despite the insecurities and fears that will arise. Embracing these higher qualities of humankind—patience, perseverance, compassion, acceptance—grant us the reward of living the deepest possible experience of life. Those willing to live life deeply will embark on the journey. You other people can stop reading here.

★ We have something that is uniquely our own to say, depict, or demonstrate, and thus we contribute variation, interest, and new dimension to the world.

★ There is an audience for our art, writing, or other creation no matter what form it takes. Finding what channel of expression is uniquely ours gives us creative flow and flight if we do not compare ourselves with what and how others have chosen to express themselves.

★ If we are working with who we truly are in our own way, comparison becomes unimportant.

★ The process of creativity produces optimal conditions for being alive. As we create, our minds and bodies are their most energetic, stay vital, and even heal.

ENTERING THE GARDEN OF THE ILLUSTRIOUS MUSES

Enter the Garden and pass a still and peaceful pool. Take a moment to gaze into its waters to see your reflection. Although it is often a mystery, and sometimes confounding, there are conditions that make creativity more attainable. Let your reflection register this and if you like, act a little cocky about the whole thing.

An Exercise Where You Get to Circle Things

Close your eyes and move into your body. Relax your muscles, take three deep let-go breaths, and quiet the mind. Then, (open your eyes), read through the following list and check anything that gives you a sense of excitement. If you have been out of touch with your intuition for a while, it will be a subtle sense, but listen carefully. This is the center from which your wisest counsel comes-your connection to the guidance from inside us. Then, if you still have no passion sense, keep reading and the Muses will direct you. Passions have a way of resurfacing on this journey. Keep an eye, an ear, and a hand out.

Circle what calls to you. Then break down some of what you have circled to small experiential pieces and sample them in abbreviated form to see where they take you.

Authentically Expressing Who You Are in Your Daily Approach to Your Life
Finding a Satisfying Creative Outlet
Art
Painting
Collage
Drawing
Multimedia
Sculpture
Ceramics
Jewelry Making
Beading
Music
Dance
Writing
Performance Art
Theater
Art Appreciation

Your Relationship with Yourself
Your Relationship with a Partner
Your Relationship to Any Others
Volunteer Work
Event Planning
Creating Winning Attitudes
In Making Everyday Life a Little More Festive and Enjoyable
In Relationship to Your Environment
Decorating
Making Sacred Spaces
Gardening
Organizing
Your Work:
Your Attitude Toward Work
New Ideas to Improve Your Work
Follow Through with Ideas You've Had in Marketing What You Do

Other Arts or Crafts	In Team Building
Hobbies	In Finding Joy in Your Job
Filmmaking	Sports
Public Speaking	Cooking
Returning to a Creative Outlet You Had Earlier in Your Life	Baking
	Socializing
Coming Up with Ideas About Anything	Vacations and Traveling
Increasing Your Intuition	Family Outing and Get-Togethers
Meditation	Being Silly
Solitude	Other:
Other:	More Other:
Also:	And Don't Forget:

Childhood Private-Eye Work

What we were drawn toward when we were little has important clues and significance for our life as an adult. There are as many dreams, dispositions, and personalities as there are children. All children are not drawn toward the same thing.

Revisiting childhood memories can give you some clues about where to focus creative energy if you have lost your connection with your true self.

Go back to your childhood and Quick List in your journal all of the things you wished to be and what kinds of things you liked to do. Can you remember what filled your little body with excitement? Be like a detective.

Find the clues for the passion waiting for your attention now. Some of them may speak very loudly. Free-associate what pursuits could be related to what you loved as a child. You may not be able to remember everything right away but opening to this listing experience oils the memory centers, and little by little more may come back to you than you think is possible. No need to remember stuff perfectly. Know that passion comes with confidence and confidence comes with practice.

Continue on the illustrious path of your dream taking <u>very tiny steps</u>. "Tiny" can be imaging what you do next, asking a question, setting up your space while you listen to one song. The paradox is, once started, you may not want to stop and will get further than if you set out to write or make art for an hour or more.

Equipment Needed for the Journey

Persistence: One of the most potent indicators of success in the creative process, is staying with it no matter what. You may feel like throwing in the towel, that's part of the process; when you don't the towel will morph into a flag of triumph.

Joy: Do you know how to feel joy? Just ask that question, nothing more.

Trust: Trust is infinitely more helpful in the manifestation of creative power than fear. Fear is normal but if you feed your trust, you can embarrass it out of bothering you too much. You may have to start small if trust is foreign but when you build trust you magnetize dreams—maybe not exactly like your initial vision but possibly in a form more consistent to your true nature. Start by simply asking without needing an answer: "What would it feel to trust my ideas? And to know that wherever they lead, even if it's different from my plan, I will adapt and triumph?" Asking questions programs your subconscious.

Patience: Impatience is a detriment to the creative process and to living an artful life, but it's not uncommon these days, so we need to work around it. Most growth processes do not happen quickly. Most take longer than you thought. Creative change takes time, compassion, and perseverance.

Focus: Focus takes practice. When the mind is all over the place—distracted by the internet, worrying about this, planning that, judging everyone and you—it is not focusing. Get a buddy and work at the same time, set a timer, break it down to five minutes, but if you find you love distractions, reward yourself with one after five minutes of focus, only if you want to. You may not want to once you get started.

Confidence: A key ingredient to creativity is confidence. With disciplined practice, the power of confidence comes alive. Acting like you are confident is a lot like *being* confident.

Solitude: Willingness to spend time alone is also indispensable to the creative process. To expand creatively we must be willing to be intimate with ourselves, to release external distractions and to listen to our inner voice. As we get to know who we are without other people, we find our unique voice and know who this self is that wants to be expressed.

Accept Help: And then there's time when reaching out, asking for feedback, and sharing what you are doing results in going where you may not have realized is a good place for you to go.

That's all the equipment you need; now it is time to meet the Muses.

A Muse Primer

The Muses of classical Greece were the daughters of Zeus, king of the gods, and Mnemosyne, goddess of memory. Their mission was to inspire mortals to creative art, writing, theater, and science. They met with major obstacles when they kept using the same old devices with the modern mortal. Distraction, avoidance techniques, and fears rendered the Muses ineffective. They have had to upgrade their approach, personalities, focus, and hobbies to get the attention and cooperation of the modern mortal.

Greek mythology tells us there were nine Muses, each a custodian of a different art. The keepers of the sciences were Clio and Urania, the Muses of history and astronomy, respectively. Terpsichore was the Muse of dance. Calliope was the eldest of the Muses, the Muse of heroic and epic poetry. Erato, was the Muse of love poetry. Euterpe's symbol was the flute, and she was the goddess of instrumental music and lyric poetry. Her sister Polyhymnia was the muse of vocal music. Melpomene was the muse of tragedy, while Thalia was the muse of comedy.

You are about to meet their modern day equivalents. Well, maybe not equivalents, but some personas whose very mission in life is to inspire self-talk, thought, and action to unleash your creativity in ways that have now been test-driven since this book first came out 20 years ago.

The Illustrious Garden of the Amazing Muses

(AND THE BODYGUARD)

The Bodyguard

When you start to get serious about this creativity thing, you may feel the reality of being alone, overwhelmed, or prone to discouragement. Or you might feel initially exhilarated and then hit the dark night of the creative soul: creative chaos, and question your sanity. These things happen naturally in the creative process. If you're human, they happen to you. If you're AI… you may have an easier time but we can tell you're not real.

How do you start the dream with all the scary things lurking out there to stop you? I'll make a suggestion: You consider the scope of your fear, but advance forward anyhow, realizing that being true to your idea is essential to your happiness because you may have obstacles, but the call won't go away.

You may see someone else doing exactly what it is you want to do, only they are further along in the process and you feel an attack of envy. The toxic stuff can stain your best intentions. Muster up courage, and simply say, "That's okay, I'm still going to do it." If that's too hard, try to embrace that idea just 5%.

There are plenty of things to discourage creativity. Don't feel like you're alone if you come up against seven or eight of them.

You Can Do It

To help out, the Modern Day Muses have assigned you a Bodyguard. He, she, they, it (we will refer to it as "it" to save space) is in the Garden of Your Creativity. You shouldn't be surprised, it's in the title of the book. The Bodyguard, however you identity its manifestation, is here to protect you from all of these adversaries of the creative process—the traitors to you unfolding as someone with a creative contribution. Your Bodyguard will be with you throughout the journey, so the Muses want you to meet it now and use the powers as your own.

Summon the Bodyguard:

- Anytime you are feeling creatively discouraged or fearful.

- When you need to be reminded that you have an inner strength that can overcome any odds.

- To unleash your best defense: your arsenal of passion and desire for your creative dream.

The Bodyguard persona mobilizes fantasy and mirth to instantly call upon a tangible image of protection. An image of a Bodyguard can be easier to employ than the abstract qualities of bravado, patience, or will. This energy prevents us from giving our power away to others. No need for this to be perfect, it takes practice. We will replace feelings of fear, discouragement, disregard, disillusionment, and frustration with confident determination. And just reading this above paragraph every now and then, can snap you out of any flailing, weak place so… REMEMBER TO DO THAT.

The Bodyguard Selection

Mortals need valiant protection against discouraging forces. The Muses themselves are not in the business of protection. They are in the business of inspiring gestures of moving ahead. Plus, they don't work out at the gym. So, they proposed the Bodyguard Act, which stipulates that Mortals Will Be Supplied with a Full- fledged Bodyguard for the Thwarting of any Evil Force That Prevents the Expression of Creative Good. The bill passed the Mount Olympus congress and the populace gasped with awe due to its controversial nature. The Muses didn't care. They are of the creative bent— avant-garde invention is their forte. Ultimately the Mount Olympians dismissed the eccentricity of the Muses saying, "Oh, well, I guess they can add bodyguards and stuff like that. They're artists, and artists break rules."

The Muses encourage you to come up with an image, a gesture, a statement that will help you embody a sense of protection that empowers persistence.

Your Bodyguard Energy

Nothing and no one can make sure that the creative side of your existence is honored except you. This is both ironic and understandable. You are born with a creative destiny. Fulfilling that destiny places you in a process of both the highest human potential and highest mortal fulfillment. But it's kind of frightening. You get to prove your commitment to creativity by overcoming the odds of being discouraged. A little help wouldn't hurt, even if it's conjured up by your imagination.

The Bodyguard's Protection Techniques

The most powerful defense against quitting or discouragement is the strength of your passionate desire. Passion comes from confidence and confidence comes from practice. So persist with practicing until you feel invincible, (within reason).

Here are other strategies:

The Anchor

The Anchor is powerful. This is the use of some thought, sensation, or movement that you can access when you feel discouraged. It is a touchstone of strength. Mostly it takes the part of our mind that torments you and replaces it with the thought or the feeling you need in order to continue full speed ahead. Or if you're not in full speed mode, even hobbling along is better than discouragement.

Anchors can be thoughts of people who empower us, music that soothes or inspires us, memories of situations that have empowered us, focusing on the nurturing nature of breathing and releasing our plight with the exhale. As usual, this takes practice and maintenance. Anchors aweigh!

Self-Talk That Serves as Anchors

So what, I'll do it anyway.

I got this.

I don't need to perfect, just to enjoy the process.

Take one small step and follow where the intuition leads.

Keep going.

What would it feel like to believe in my process?

What's worked in the past?

(Think of ones that have worked for you in the past.)

What else works for you?

Questions to Ask Yourself to Activate Bodyguard Powers:

- What anchor empowers me to protect and stay committed to my creative process?
- What does it feel like to use this anchor?
- When and how can I remember to use it?
- What does passionate commitment look like and feel like to me? When did I experience it in the past?
- What example of someone else's success can I remember to empower commitment toward my own?
- Can I remember that I can be imperfect at activating my Bodyguard Powers and still succeed…brilliantly?
- What would I do if I felt just 15% more courage about staying with my idea?
- What would I be like if I just didn't listen to doubting voices and skeptical detractors?

Suggestions:
> Make a shield out of poster board or what have you and add anchors, images, quotes and role-models on it… hang it where you can see it or mentally absorb it.

THE BRUSH-OFF

This is the Bodyguard's simple but incredibly effective technique to release either your own negative thoughts as they arise, or the discouraging comments of others.

Here is how it works: Upon catching yourself thinking a negative or antagonizing thought, or being "accosted" by someone else's derailing comment or facial expression of criticism, simply take your hands and physically brush the thought or comment off your body as if you were getting rid of dirt or bugs. Try it right now. The physical action combined with the intention to remove negative energy somehow works better than just the thought of trying to ignore or to get over the situation.

CREATIVITY OFFENDERS

The Bodyguard's energy is a solid stock of your belief in yourself. It will protect you from these antagonists to the creative process:

- Fear
- Discouragement in any form
- The desire to quit
- Envy of others
- Others envying and neglecting you
- Jealousy from you and of you
- Unworthy criticism
- Disheartening criticism
- Ridicule, mockery, shaming, and really weird looks from people
- Rationalizations about not having enough time
- Thoughts about what we think we should be doing instead of creativity
- Partners who don't respect your creative needs, space, and time

- Your guilt about taking your creative space and time
- Unfounded self-doubt
- Gravitation toward TV reruns
- Checking the e-mail every fifteen minutes
- Veers left when your creativity is on the right
- Fright, terror, heebie-jeebies
- Superficial socializing as an avoidance strategy
- Giving your power away
- And the pull of oblivion

The Bodyguard's Reinforcements to Thwart Creative Enemies

Be advised: the Bodyguard is tougher than the Muses. Some ruthlessness may need to be employed to keep you loyal to your creative call.

Discouragement in Any Form

When you are discouraged to the point of wanting to quit, know that you're not alone ... it's part of the creative process to feel hindered every now and then. It is those who persist, who triumph, not only in their creative work, but the muscle developed makes staying-power easier in other parts of life. Stymie that desire to quit with relaxed focused action instead. Use compassion, patience, and self-love. These may seem like soft qualities, but they result in strength, coping skills, and resilience. Start really small until you can let the passionate flow lift and carry you. (Really small can be 30 seconds, one page, point yourself in the direction of your work.) Realize the power of practice, patience, and perseverance. You're allowed to feel discouraged; you're not allowed to stop unless it's a brief break.

JEALOUSY AND ENVY

When feeling jealousy and envy, again… know that these qualities come with being human. Identify what these emotions are telling you about what you may be neglecting in your life. Start that action, again with tiny steps, with patience. Or if that does not apply, engage in a creative activity that reinforces the magnificence of your gifts. Get back to who you are as an amazing mortal, and what others are doing won't matter as much. No need to do this perfectly; believe it a little at a time. Say, "So what… I'll do it anyway." Jealousy is a message that there is some work you might want to get to, but start or continue it with small, fun steps. Or it could be something that was installed from childhood or genes, so accept it and then become bigger than it.

CRITICISM

When you receive unworthy or disheartening criticism from people who may be jealous of you or who are just unconscious of what they are saying, take your power back. Love them from afar but free them from your life even if it's temporarily. Do not give your power to others. Be conscious when you do give your power away. You need that power in your court to keep you going, and for your creative long-run. Once you hand your power over to the opinions of others, you are at the mercy of an unconquerable force. If you have been deeply true to your creativity, (and yourself) you will have both admirers and critics. Strength and self-confidence are the ingredients of your creative freedom.

Discern if the criticism is helpful. Be honest with yourself. Is there a nugget of truth from which you can benefit? There's usually an intuitive hit that something is useful; it may not always be easy to hear but gently consider how you might use it.

NO TIME

You have time for what you choose to have time for. Recognize anything that stops you from your creative work that could be an excuse. It's often easier to use the "not enough time" excuse than to face the music, so to speak. Surely, there are things that normally steal our time, but creativity is not meant for your spare time. Creative moments are possible every day even if it's simply asking yourself questions: What small step will I take next? What design? Color? Character? Direction?

Assess where you are spending your time now. Admit if you are addicted to TV, the Internet or other distractions and find some structure as in classes, creativity coaching or parallel universe time (working at the same time as your buddy). Set a timer when you're on the Internet, one that's in another room so you have to get up to turn it off. Have an inner bodyguard that is kind and compassionate helping you guard against these things.

Thoughts About What We Think We Should Be Doing Instead of Creativity

Hoodwinked by shoulds? If you "should" be doing everything but your creativity, redefine your values; they may not be in line with your value of having creativity in your life. Doing five minutes in the morning of your creative pursuit can have a profound effect on the rest of your day… and life.

Guilt About Taking Your Creative Space and Time

Guilt and worry come with being human and often with what we were taught as children. They can become habits that spoil or delay our creative efforts. However, there are many successful creative people who do not subscribe to guilt's interference. Do you have role models who do not feel guilty? Thinking of them may be the permission you need.

Mortal Examples

These mortals could have been thwarted by public opinion or failures. Instead, they protected their dream by staying with it despite the odds. The Bodyguard guards against giving up.

- ❀ Dr. Seuss's first book was rejected forty-five times.
- ❀ JFK finished last in his Ivy League college.
- ❀ Charles Schulz was rejected by Disney.
- ❀ Buckminster Fuller, inventor of the geodesic dome, was expelled twice from Harvard.
- ❀ Jack Nicholson, Marilyn Monroe, John Travolta, and many more actors who became superstars were told they couldn't act.

Stay committed to your heart's journey. Know that you are not alone. Call upon your inner strength. Surpass your own expectations.

Modern Day Examples of Bodyguards

People who seemed to have a protective force helping them: Ruth Bader Ginsberg, Frida Kahlo, Dolly Parton, anyone with a disability who persists anyway, characters from movies who inspire you. It was a long time ago, but Jody Foster's character from the movie Contact inspired me.

Enter the Garden

A Muse is there to greet you at the garden's entrance. See before you a goddess of light or in this case, lightbulbs. She leads you to the garden gate. Looking over the gate and into the garden, your awareness shifts vividly into the present moment. She summons you to walk through the gate and you can't refuse because you sense there is something you need to know for your creativity. Through this gate you see flashes of insight, the pure, uncut rapture of creative enlightenment. The moment is alive—there are new possibilities. Her lightbulbs are the beacons of new ideas. You follow their glow and feel a little . . . lighter.

The Muse has turned off interruptions from the noisy voices of worry and distraction. Preoccupations of future and past, the disruption of rehearsed conversation, guilt or regrets, judgment or self-criticism, are muted. The mind then opens like the curtains of a movie screen. You realize you have the ability to connect to the mind's fleeting electricity, which creates stories, rhymes, rhythms, insights, and visions, including one of you as a freely expressed agent of creativity.

The world is a smorgasbord of ideas waiting for your selection. Driving becomes a time where ideas billboard your attention. Taking a bath becomes a reservoir of bubbling ideas. As you work in the kitchen, new ideas spontaneously brew. These flashes awaken you. They open the senses right here and now making the creative process possible . . . making the theater of the mind a blessing within your reach. But you must consciously pay attention, even if it's just for 15 seconds at a time.

ENTER THE GARDEN.

AHA - PHRODITE:
MUSE OF PAYING ATTENTION, PASSION, AND POSSIBILITIES

If I have ever made any valuable discoveries,
it has been owing more to patient attention,
than any other talent. —Isaac Newton, mathematician

SUMMON AHA-PHRODITE

◎ To wake up to the inspiration all around you.

◎ To use the power of passionate attention-paying for your creativity.

◎ To capture and savor your inspiration.

Bottom Line

If we pay attention to the present moment, we will discover that inspiration is not elusive or out of reach. An unfathomable amount of inspiration is already right in front of us. We may have to tweak HOW we pay attention, but voltage is everywhere, and we when we connect to the electricity of our awareness, anything in our environment can become a conductor of new ideas. Everything from the way the light dances on a bird's feathers to the music in a child's laughter can become the art of our lives and the substance of artistic expression. In this consciousness, the passion for the creative process is irresistible.

Paying attention is (1) feeling awake and alive to creative possibility; (2) being fully conscious as a gentle witness to and passionate connoisseur of all of life's offerings; (3) noticing who we already are as unique creative souls.

But paying attention is also moving beyond the tendency to default to negativity and direct our attention to those things that work for us, those that have worked for us in the past, and our strengths and uniqueness. This choice will empower our desire and confidence to be creative and comes from a simple shift in our attention.

The Selection of Aha-phrodite

The nine Greek Muses were sitting around chattering in the Muse brainstorm chamber. As they began the selection process, lightning flashed from their ideas. "What New Muse Transformations Do We Need to Make in Order to Jump-Start the Creatively Destined Modern Day Mortal Mind?" That was the question the Muses wrote on their Muse Dry Erase Brainstorm Board.

They decided that the first Muse named should be representative of both the Muses in ancient Greek mythology and the newly upgraded Modern Day Muses. Polyhymnia (she of many hymns) exclaimed, "Aha!" and the rest of them agreed. Thus, Aha-phrodite was named.

Aha-phrodite's name was inspired from Aphrodite, goddess of love and beauty and well-known daughter of Zeus and Hera. The "Aha" portion of the name was gleaned, of course, from the exclamation "Aha!" that happens with the discovery of a new idea. It was then combined with the old Greek name stem phrodite, from Aphrodite, making the new name a combination of both old and new, and of passion and discovery. This, they believed, was not only politically correct but rather clever as well.

Your Aha-phrodite Energy

Aha-phrodite energy is about the power of paying attention to the rapture of ideas and all else that may play into supporting creative output as well as enjoying life.

Here are some examples from Aha-phrodite herself:

- ❀ Where will I find inspiration today?
- ❀ What in this moment is imbibed with beauty, art, or curiosity?
- ❀ What will reveal itself today that will inspire in me a new idea?
- ❀ What have I already started that I can continue to cultivate for creativity?

It is important to capture ideas as they occur since ideas are fleeting. Aha-phrodite's main plea to you is this: "When an idea arrives, write it down!"

The aim of life is to live, and to live means to be aware, joyously, drunkenly, serenely, divinely aware.
~ Henry Miller, novelist

Aha-phrodite's Energy Detector

One way of paying attention is to notice what energizes you. Begin to be a keen observer of your energy meter. What seems to make you feel more awake?

What perks your ears up? Make a list of all your ideas and audition them based on which sparks the most intuitive energy.

What makes you stop the autopilot daily routine and energizes you? This is a divining rod leading you to where you will excel the most. That energy will help hurtle you past the obstacle that may come up for you in the process.

If you have difficulty paying attention to one of your ideas, narrow them down to the top three - like judges from a reality talent show might do. Three is a good number to work on at once versus seventeen or 389.

Can you make paying attention a game? Take a walk and take away the label of things, notice shapes, designs, and patterns. What do you find pleasing or artistic? This is paying attention calisthenics and you will notice it begins to show up in other areas of your life.

Muse Profile of Aha-phrodite

Symbol

A lightbulb with wings symbolizes an idea taking flight. Aha-phrodite turns on by enlightening awareness and shifting attention to this idea's capacity to bring something new into existence.

> True passion is intoxicating and invigorating, soothing and sensuous, magical and mystical. I just thought you should know what you're in for.
> ~ Tazo tea bag: "Passion"

Ritual to Summon Aha-phrodite

To summon Aha-phrodite: Fill a page of your sketchbook or journal with a drawing of a lightbulb. Freely write ideas that come to mind about artfully living a life, or about your specific creative passion. Don't worry about making sense, just fit random thoughts inside the bulb to ignite your brilliance. Or color the lightbulb with designs and shapes using crayons, colored pencils, markers, watercolors, or oil pastels. Coloring within a contained spaced can center us, giving us practice paying attention to one thing at a time.

Under the lightbulb write: "I honor Aha-phrodite's presence in my life by having notepads, journals, sketchpads, or tape-recording devices ready wherever I am, in order to catch inspiration's possibilities." Sign your name with love. Say one of the affirmations or ask one of the questions listed below. Watch for inspiration.

AHA-PHRODITE AFFIRMATIONS AND SMALL QUESTIONS

- What if I awaken to the inspiration that surrounds me more regularly?
- How will I remember to pay attention to idea triggers and the light in the world?
- Where can I direct my attention that it will both serve my creativity and my joy?
- What do I say to myself that results in inspiration or desire to get to my creative pursuits?
- I collect ideas as they come to me and cultivate their possibilities.
- Something creative is about the happen.

And there you have it. Your Aha-phrodite energy is awakened. Don't forget to remember it.

JOURNAL CHECK-IN

1. Take out your journal and write about where you are with your Aha-phrodite energy. What were you thinking about yourself as you read the chapter? What aspects of creativity are you passionate about? Keep going with this unfinished sentence or fill it in differently five or six time: When I pay attention…

2. Make a list of where you've been paying attention lately. First list anything that comes to mind. Put an x by anything that is judgmental or a worry – and if there isn't any of those on your list, think if you've been judgmental or have had worries and add them, knowing they come with being human and that's okay. Put a heart by anything on your list that feels good to pay attention to, or add things if there were some you just haven't listed yet. Add another list of what you'd like to pay more attention to. Making this list turns up the volume of your attention; the trick is to be a benevolent witness to it all.

3. Successful writers, comedians, poets keep a notebook of things that happen during the day, so Aha-phrodite encourages you to do the same. Pat yourself on the back if you do this already. Have something you use to record funny and interesting moments and ideas.

4. Take a few deep let-go breaths. Write a letter to yourself from Aha-phrodite. Let her give you some specifics and encouragement about paying attention and the possibilities in each new day. Let her praise you for what you are doing now.

5. Notice what works for you lately, where you are "getting it right," and pay attention to what has worked for you in the past. These empower your strengths and confidence which lead to more enjoyment of creativity and life.

Muse Walk—Aha-phrodite Style

Go out for a walk and fill in the blank as often as possible: I notice…

Pair walking with the asking of small questions. Believe that on your walk there may be some inspiration, in a form you do not need to know, awaiting your attention.

Pay attention to different themes: notice everywhere yellow shows up, horizontal and vertical patterns, things you wouldn't notice if you weren't paying attention.

Prerequisite to Catching a Dream:

Finding The Jewels Of Delight

Every day we are blessed with dozens of experiences capable of bringing us delight. We notice some of them with only partial awareness if at all. Fuller awareness of these little instances of enjoyment will give us regular jolts of appreciation. This new awareness allows our desire for always needing "more" to disappear at the same time abundance begins to fill our lives. Like everything, it takes practice.

When you notice, try expanding the experience and dislodging from the habitual trance, but extending your enjoyment of it for just five seconds longer. After a while your quality of attention will deepen.

Jewels Of Delight

Here are some examples: the first light in the morning, seeing a jumping dolphin, unexpected humor that makes you burst with laughter, having no one sit beside you on the airplane so you can stretch out, the feel of clean sheets (especially with shaved legs), the smell of coffee, the first exciting moments of a road trip, coming home after a long trip, saying something brilliantly funny at the right time, good friends having dinner together, putting on clothes that have just come out of the dryer on a cold morning, stepping into a warm car after feeling chilled, the look of someone who appreciated your unexpected help, the day you feel better after having been sick for a while, putting on jeans that feel looser than the last time you wore them, the bite of the first juicy nectarine of the summer, a flock of birds in flight, Sunday mornings, holding hands, running into a good friend, knowing you are about to see a great movie, a breeze, the wonder of a perfectly formed flower.

These are the ingredients of moments of fulfillment. If you cannot connect to the delight in these simple things, you will be unprepared to feel deeply what are considered big delights, successes, and accomplishments in life.

Take out your journal and Quick List twenty jewels of delight now. Or even better, have a list on which you can regularly add more jewels. They become a mood-lifter or antidepressant when you have the blues. They regularly reinforce the splendor of your existence. After listing, notice that you begin to experience more of them spontaneously because you have put activated radar for increased joy-detecting frequency.

YOU MUST BE PRESENT TO WIN

Idea Bank

Once you have established the habit of carrying idea-catching materials, Aha-phrodite will comply by producing even more ideas. She's good like that. As you catch all these ideas, consider starting an Idea Bank where you can deposit your notes. The Idea Bank could be a file folder on your computer, shoebox, desk drawer, an electronic device, or a card index box. You could collect ideas in Pinterest or an online journal. If you are an avid journal writer, stick notes that you caught outside of journal-writing time in your journal with tape or Post-its. Other material can be added to your bank or journal such as newspaper clippings, cartoons, quotes, or helpful hints.

Sometimes in my journal writing, viable ideas for projects, writing, or art will spring out of my daily dribble. It is important for me to circle or highlight these ideas so I can easily find them amidst all the other writing.

The Next Stop in the Garden

On the path through the garden you come across a male figure. He is beside a chalkboard wildly scrawling words and pictures, lists and flow charts, doodles and hieroglyphics. He's having a good time. You have wanted to be more resourceful in your creative process, to prolifically spawn new ideas or new ways to look at things. This guy greets you and in a German accent he says:

"Your mind can be scho much greater den mediocre. Just tweet a little here, reverse a little dere, imagine schome more under dis, schimmy a vord or two into somesching new, and ve schall see new ideas zat vill bring newness, novelty, and miracles. Ve have definite vays of being mysteriously schpectaclar. It's all in za thinking ... so just think you can think somesching new and zen vatch the fireverks."

ALBERT:

Muse of Imagination and Innovation

There are only two ways to live your life.
One is as though nothing is a miracle.
The other is as though everything is a miracle.
~ Albert Einstein

Summon Albert When

- You want to find new ways of thinking for joy and creativity.

- You want more creative resourcefulness.

- You want to enrich your imagination.

- You want to question existing parameters and "break the rules" in the name of creativity, innovation, and the occasional miracle.

Bottom Line

We have the power to think differently about our lives as well as *about* creative thinking. If we look at the same thing everyone else sees and think something different, we have just become creative. When we can fluidly list a myriad of ideas, we are innovative. When we plug into that place inside that can invent a world filled with intuitive symbols and spontaneous wisdom, we are imaginative.

We can choose thoughts that change the way we feel that then change the way we act that change our destiny. Now ZAT is creativity. In choosing creative thought, we create a deeper level of existence and a continual resource of ideas, solutions, and attitudes that best reflect the unfolding of our authentic self. What we previously defined as mundane can be an element of the amazing. Our lives fill with the magic that possibility thinking can create. This is the physics of fulfillment.

The Selection of Albert

"What do mortals need next?" thought the Muses about the continuing inspirational upgrade they were executing. They thought and thought and thought, and then they decided to stop thinking because it was getting monotonous. They had to change HOW they were thinking. They started experimenting with words, sounds, images, associations, mirrors, and fusion. And new thoughts started percolating.

Soon afterward they said, "Okay, enough already. Let's quit dawdling." They were just stalling because stalling is an unexpected thing for a Muse to do. And that is what the next Muse is all about. He is about defying the obvious for the innovative. He inspires mortals to see with new eyes so that what they were used to seeing one way can be construed in a much different way.

To get into the spirit of this Muse, protocols were broken and boundaries were stretched. Thus, this Muse is a male instead of a female. Not only that, but a mortal also inspired the selection of this Muse in a realm where Muses usually inspire mortals. They laughed at this disobedient gesture of pure genius, and then I can't remember which one, but one of them said, "Well, we've got to throw in some surprises or else the mortal mind will stall in complacency when it could be cruising in possibility."

The next Muse is named and modeled after a mortal icon of innovation, imagination, and revolutionary thinking. Albert Einstein broke the rules, revered imagination, and believed that we had a choice to live life as if it were a full-blown miracle. Thus, we have Albert the Muse.

Your Albert Energy

To infinity and beyond!
~ Buzz Lightyear, Toy Story

Albert is the catalyst for original thinking, the corner stone both of creativity and seeing life's difficulties in a way that makes them easier. The use of his energy can expand a mortal's world into a new reality. When mortals allow their consciousness to move beyond what they had previously thought possible, they can relinquish old, tired, discouraging styles of thinking and shift to an unbounded existence.

Albert encourages mortals to bypass obvious solutions and venture into the ingenious, to continue beyond the first and find several new ideas so that a more informed selection can be made. How exciting to think mortals can move beyond automatic "default thinking" to "possibility thinking." Possibility thinking enables mortals to be more alive, as well as to invent, be resourceful, solve problems easily, and forge into dazzling and brilliant new realms of expression.

Thinking Differently About Thinking

> No problem can be solved from the same consciousness that created it.
> ~ Albert Einstein

Let's step into a new consciousness. According to studies, we use a small percentage of our brain's true potential. And generally speaking, we do not do too badly as a species just using that much. We hear these studies, but none of them ever say HOW to use more of the brain's potential. Enter Albert. Can you imagine how different our lives would be if we used just thirty percent more of this magnificent organ we have?

Breaking the Rules

There are all sorts of ways to begin using more of our brains to deepen and brighten the experience of our life. The first one is to question the existing rules.

> "Learn the rules like a pro, so you can break them like an artist."
> ~ Pablo Picasso

Albert Einstein won a Nobel Prize for his work on relativity. He broke the rules of physics that, until his time in history, were considered unchangeable. His deviation out of existing parameters proves that rules can be broken and that enormous advances in science are possible. Thus, the Muses believe his example can motivate anyone who wants to make even small advances in their creativity. The Muse Albert illustrates one of his tools of innovation, the "tool of association between two unrelated ideas".

The Modern-Day Muse Albert's New Theories of Relativity

- You will enjoy life relative to how much you are inclined to think about life in a way that makes it worth enjoying.

- You are creative relative to whether you think you are creative or not.

- You will come up with new ideas when you relate two or more formerly unrelated objects, notions, images, or words. This is the foundation of innovation, humor, new products, novel concepts, and Reese's peanut butter cups.

- Myriad possibilities are relatively easier to discover than you may think.

When we do find new ways to live, we create another dimension in which to express ourselves, to live life more deeply, and to inspire others to do the same. So then, why do we insist on following the narrowly contrived rules of others?

Never Stop Questioning

When I host art and writing workshops, I add this instruction after the original instructions: "Or however you want to do it, there is no right or wrong, this is a *creativity* class." Participants are encouraged to break the rules so that something new has a chance to be discovered. Most students have a hard time actually following through with this instruction. Some feel absolutely liberated breaking the rules, and still others are uncomfortable with such an open structure.

Next time you embark on a creative endeavor, look at the instructions through a different lens—see how you can change them to better accommodate your individual style and expression. Start with chicken salad.

Curiosity and Wonder

"I have no special talents. I am only passionately curious."
~ Albert Einstein ... again

Brainfeast:
A Banquet of Idea-Generating Techniques

In the following sections, Albert shall reawaken the center of the mortal mind where ingenuity resides. Just open your mind and say, "Awe!"

The Physics of New Ideas

Listing: The Muses have you listing throughout the book because it is one of the most effective ways to forge new literal pathways in the brain through which more ideas can flow. Listing helps us go beyond the first five obvious. Searching hard for fifteen to forty-five more ideas flexes muscles of idea fluidity.

Listing also alerts the subconscious to keep going with the subject even after you've stopped putting your list on paper. More ideas will spontaneously present themselves in the weeks ahead. Then the resourcefulness you are developing will begin to happen naturally in every aspect of both art and life. You will surprise yourself at the number of ideas that begin to accompany your every day.

To **Quick List**, number your paper to the specified number in each exercise, or to at least twenty. (If you want to really EXPAND your mind's capacity to easily generate ideas, go as long as you can.) Then, according to the focus indicated in the exercise, begin listing without stopping to think. If you cannot think of the next item to write on the list, repeat yourself, write gibberish, write complaints about the exercise itself, but keep writing. This method prevents you from prejudging thoughts and getting stuck. The point is to open the brain's ability to run free without worries or distractions. Often unexpected clever stuff emerges.

Associations: Associations are used as a way to generate new ideas. This process starts by ascribing new meanings to existing concepts. Existing words, images, sensations, thoughts, or concepts can elicit new ideas that are triggered by loosely associating new meanings to parts of old concepts. Imagine how things you see and hear can be construed as something else and that muscle in your mind will entertain you more than any TV show is capable of doing.

> Since my childhood I have been creative in weird ways.
> When I see a gadget, say a blender,
> I imagine how I can use it for something else.
> ~ Isabel Allende

Connections: This is the connection of two previously unconnected words, images, senses, thoughts, or concepts. Try relating cooking to dancing, birds to designing a garden, random verbs to art ideas. You will find more on this in the Brainstorm.

Repetition: This is the creative potential elicited by repeating a word, image, sound, or concept over and over (and over). Rhythm, punch, and artistic tension are created with the throb, throb, throb of bold repetition. The mind will volunteer words and ideas in the midst of repetition because it responds to the spontaneous fill-in the blank structure. For instance, repetitively fill in the sentence: I can think differently by . . . Listen to the rhythms in spoken word poetry and then adopt that rhythm for your own words.

Personification: Bring a concept to life by giving it a personality. The Muses are proud to be an example of this concept. What if your best qualities were personified? Would you take them to lunch?

Relocation: Getting up from your desk and relocating your body someplace else will also relocate your mind out of a limited groove. Moving, working from a café, in an auditorium, or even talking while standing will create many more ideas, techniques, and solutions than sitting. I generate richer ideas while talking in class or talking in front of my sink than while sitting at my desk.

Exaggeration: We operate in a narrow range of expression to be socially appropriate. This limits our awareness of ranges past daily acceptability that are filled with new ideas and more artistic methods of expression. Many times, exaggerating an idea, a concept, a dance move, an art approach, a story, or a problem in need of solution can take it to a new level of energy or create new insights by removing it from its designated space. Make it really big, small, dramatic, angry, nice, etc. This breaks you out of a formerly limited range of thought and expression.

Take a problem in your life at present. In your journal exaggerate it way out of proportion. Dramatize your reactions to it. Create new characters if you feel the need. Bring in your own special spirit guides to help out. Invite background singers, firemen, the clergy, police, superheroes, characters from different movies, to join you.

What in your life can you minimize? Talk about an important event nonchalantly- see if it gives you new insights or at the very least, relaxes you.

More Thoughts About Thinking Differently

> The real voyage of discovery consists not in
> seeking new landscapes but in having new eyes.
> ~ Marcel Proust

> A rock pile ceases to be a rock pile the moment a single man contemplates it,
> bearing within him the image of a cathedral.
> ~ Antoine de Saint-Exupery

Muse Profile of Albert

Symbol

Albert's symbol is a box falling open releasing the wonder of new possibilities. This happens when we choose to shift our mind's focus to the possibilities outside of the usual predictably packaged thinking.

> Take the obvious, add a cupful of brains, a generous pinch of imagination,
> a bucketful of courage and daring, stir well, and bring to a boil.
> ~ Bernard Baruch

Affirmations and Small Questions from Albert

- I get to think new ways about my existence.
- What's one small way I can think more creatively, innovatively, or differently today?
- How can I look at something everyone else sees, and think something different?
- I generate many ideas and solutions - there is more than one right answer.
- I am open to breaking rules for creative adventure.

Journal Check-In

1. Take out your journal and write about the use of Albert's energy in your life now and where you could use more. Make it an Albert Inventory.

2. Take a few deep breaths to let go of your body's tension and your mind's chatter. Then write a letter to yourself from your Albert energy. Use your nondominant hand if you choose. Let Albert give you some pointers and encouragement on thinking differently, making up your own rules, and being resourceful. Let him counter the inner critic with anything that is needed and praise you for whatever efforts you have made so far.

Muse Walk—Albert Style

Take a walk and be in your Albert energy. Invite connections to come up for you without forcing them. Watch that your mind does not go to default thinking, and if you notice it does, gently shift to possibility thinking. What's next in your creative project, how you can break the rules, go for the less obvious. Let the walk be an opportunity to exercise different thought patterns.

Look for all the patterns, shapes, colors, and symbols on your walk. What horizontal patterns do you see? How about vertical? How does what you see on the walk connect with your creative passion? What other random thoughts do you have while walking that can connect to your creative passion? How can you think differently about this walk? What do you see that you can think differently about?

> No amount of skillful invention can replace the essential element of imagination. ~ Edward Hopper

Brainstorm
Milking the Absurd and Tuning Up Your Imagination

- Write, say, paint, dance, or act nonsensical things to move beyond the walls of your previous limitations.

- Write a completely absurd essay about what happened yesterday. Go past the boundaries of what's expected of you. Or draw, paint, or dance in an absurd way illustrating the essence of yesterday. Let this stimulate your brain expansion centers. Sometimes giving ourselves permission to be absurd results in new territories of genius.

- Imagine you are a character from one of your favorite books or movies. How do you approach your creative passion now? How do you approach lunch, your friends, your enemies?

- Imagine you are the most respected artist in the field of your creative passion and write your thoughts about having this position and what you will do with it.

- Listen to all different kinds of music; make yourself comfortable and let images arise from the music. Let the music be a soundtrack for your own personal music.

🌀 Talk spontaneously about your creative passion and what you plan on doing with it next to an imagined audience in your living room. Do the same for an imagined group of fans, an imagined group of children, an imagined group of aliens, and an imagined group of reporters.

Cultivating Resourcefulness

Associations

Humor often comes from the quick association of new meanings to old thoughts, ideas, and images. In other words, breaking the rules of a word's meaning and ascribing another meaning by some idea that comes loosely to mind from a trigger provided by the thought, idea, word, or image that goes along with the word. Whoa. Here's some humor from the Internet. Examining an existing word, ignoring its real meaning, and associating a new definition based on its spelling creates these new words:

Abdicate—(v.) to give up all hope of ever having a flat stomach.

Esplanade—(v.) to attempt an explanation while drunk.

Flabbergasted—(adj.) appalled over how much weight you have gained.

Lymph—(v.) to walk with a lisp.

Don't Settle for the First Solution

Here is one of Albert's most powerful tools. When you start playing with your ideas, make a habit of going past the first solution. Each time you start brainstorming, ask, "How can I take this a step further, and then another step further after that?" Quick Listing comes in handy here by catching your additional steps. Explore mind-mapping - Google Image it . . . and see how you can teach your mind to think differently.

Associative Word Triggers

I use the following words in my private coaching sessions to create new ideas and fun approaches to practice with artists from all disciplines. Storytellers, comedians, painters, and writers use them to come up with new ways to think about their craft. To use this technique, associate the word new ways to experiment with your creative passion. You can use the literal meaning of the word or anything the word reminds you of to come up with new ideas. Begin this practice by looking at each word and associating what ideas that word can give you for doodling or moving your body.

exaggerate	hopscotch	electrify
minimize	blow	get scared
relax	vibrate	repeat
make believe	acknowledge	make unnecessary
broadcast	circle	rearrange
reverse	belittle	start in the middle
compound	exalt	shift
invent	improve	subtract
mesmerize	plot	cut in half
improvise	over tell	exclamation point
elevate	under tell	gibber
splurge	confuse	simplify
rest	make weird	

Connections

*To me books on butterflies or baseball are more legitimate
in terms of thinking about business strategy issues.*
~ Tom Peters

Here are some examples to help illustrate the exercise of connections:

◎ Find a kitchen appliance and write a list of how it can inspire you to do your creative work differently.

◎ Open Scientific American and see what science articles can inspire art for you.

◎ Open a book, find a line, and copy it down. Add your own writing for the next several lines or until you feel you've gone far enough.

Stringing Jewels Together

Take some of your jewels of existence from Aha-phrodite's brainstorm section and newly associate them by stringing them together in a poem or verse. What you will find is poetry or prose made from the small parts of life that bring you delight. The writing will transport you into a place where pleasure resides: the well-fed mind.

Quick Listing for Increased Fluency of Thought

This is where innovation and distinction surface. Use some of the following ideas to warm up your listing skills:

- Small questions that you can constantly ask to keep your creative thinking alive. How many uses you can think of for an empty egg carton?

- Ways you can redecorate your space to reflect who you are. Ways to reorganize the food in your refrigerator.

- Ways you can generate new business (be absurd, silly, break the rules).

- Ways you can enjoy the work you do more.
- Things to do on Sundays.
- New names for yourself.
- Your favorite words.
- Constructive ways to show anger.
- Different ways to show love.
- Places you'd like to go.
- Subjects you'd like to write about, paint, sculpt, collage, act out, write a song for.
- Secret lives you'd like to live.

Wardrobe of Personas

Backup Personas

Come up with a group of personas that serve you. A persona is a different set of personality characteristics summoned to address your present situation. Using a persona is creatively adapting to your world by reinventing who you are. It is surpassing your tendency to be fearful by inventing a confident persona and then wearing it. It is moving beyond your inclination not to believe in yourself as a creative person by wearing a creative persona and then feeling more certain about your creativity. It's like putting on an outfit that better equips you for the world.

I have a friend who is relatively introverted. When she is in social situations, she rolls up her selves to indicate she is putting herself in a socially competent persona. The shift in thinking, accompanied by a symbolic change in her clothing, seems to make her more socially comfortable. Although she is the same person, believing she can be something different, and then becoming it with a developed idea, gives her a greater range of responses for the complex world—a characteristic of a creative person.

What if you had different personas to upgrade your thinking? What would they be and what could you do to indicate that they are in operation? What if you had an imaginary friend who took over when you engaged in your creative pursuits? How would he or she be different from you?

Sage Advice

What if you could get a famous and/or respected historical or present-day person to comment on your project? What would the following people or characters say about the creative solutions you are looking for? Don't be too literal. Use your imagination. Take on their persona for yourself and write or sketch from their point of view:

Abraham Lincoln, Audrey Hepburn, Bugs Bunny, Albert Einstein
Mark Twain ,e. e. cummings, Dr. Seuss
Tom Robbins, Jon Stewart, Stephen Colbert, Jerry Seinfeld
Lady Gaga
Your fairy godmother
Rumi
Your best friend
The smartest person you know
The most respected person in your life
The funniest person you know
A favorite author
Your neighbor
Owner of the minimart down the street
Lewis Carroll

Who would you include in a think-tank meeting about your creative project?

The Next Stop in the Garden

As you walk farther into the garden, the earth does a "Wordsworth"—it begins to laugh in flowers. The breeze dances in trees and you have an urge to be a little silly. Along the path, a childlike apparition beckons you to leave behind rigid, serious adult responsibilities. With her you climb through a tunnel, down a slide, over a jungle gym, (with a brief stop at an ice-cream truck), to a playground where having fun, being playful, even foolish, is encouraged. She gives you a funny cap to wear backward, a squirt gun to destroy the eminent imaginary monsters along the way, and sneakers to leap over villains. She takes your hand and says, "Let's make believe we are on another planet," "Let's invent a new language," "Let's hide behind that tree and surprise your friends when they walk by."

Pretty soon, fresh new ideas emerge like presents on Christmas morning. She takes you back to where the present moment is open with childlike wonder and uninhibited silliness. Fun is the main goal, because it creates relaxation, new visions, and the freedom to think originally and spontaneously. This Muse is here to set you free from the too-serious ties that bind you creatively . . . namely yourself as an adult. The good news here is having fun and allowing yourself to play have tremendous benefits on enhancing your creativity.

BEA SILLY:
MUSE OF PLAY,
LAUGHTER, AND DANCE

It's so much fun being human.
~ Rhonda Britten

Summon Bea Silly When

◎ You need to relearn how to play, lighten up, release rigid thinking, and remember how to make your creative expression fun.

◎ You need to remember and reawaken to the wonder of being a child and know the positive implications this has for your creativity.

◎ You are feeling resistant toward working creatively for one of these reasons:

❀ You just don't seem to want to.

❀ You feel a childlike power struggle inside you. You want to do something creative, but you never actually do it.

Bottom Line

Joy, play, laughter, and dance make life lighter and more creative. The cultivation of joy is rewarded with new ideas and fun. Let go of the rigidity of being an adult, find yourself again in play and laughter. Realize play results in productivity and is actually vital to the creative process.

The Bea Silly Selection

Bea Silly got her name from one of the earlier Modern Day Muse assignment meetings. The Muses were sitting around intensely brainstorming about various possibilities. They wore deep-furrowed brows. Thalia, the Greek Muse of comedy, noticed, "Dudes! Aren't we getting just a little bit too serious?" Knowing that this is unwise in the creative process because seriousness often chokes the play of ideas that generate handfuls of ingenuity, the Muse Albert replied, "Hey, for za next hour, let's just be silly." The experience was rewarding . . . and Bea Silly was born.

Your Bea Silly Energy

All creative people are kids at heart.
~ Steve Carmichael

Bea Silly knows that the childlike qualities mortals possess are highly responsible for their creative flow. She encourages mortals to loosen up and take creativity less seriously. She is the energy inside mortals that catalyzes play. All mortals have this energy. Yet for some, a strict, uncompromising adult side put the playful side away with the roller skates.

Fun is an elixir of spontaneous ideas. Solutions that seemed so elusive earlier appear effortlessly in the midst of play. To engage in the kind of play that stimulates ideas, mortals need to take themselves less seriously and make room for making things up, kidding, and goofing off. Bea Silly advocates the mortal prerogative to be silly, foolish, and frivolous, and thus have fun. She wants mortals to step out of the adult mode that, because of its tight adherence to unbendable rules, leaves little room for creative discoveries.

A light mind creates an inner playground for ideas. Insecurities that mortals have about letting down their adult guard, and thus looking foolish, need to be reexamined for the benefit of creative exhilaration. Who is the fool? The childlike mortal with a lightness of heart dancing with the spontaneity of mischievous ideas, or the strictly adult mortal who takes himself too seriously?

The Freedom of Childlike Activities

Are we having fun yet?
~ Carol Burnett

Sometimes I ask my classes to draw themselves doing playful things. Most students freeze up at the prospect of having to draw anything. Given permission to draw like five-year-olds, they go at it. When they are asked to scribble, miraculously they dive in with great enthusiasm—the pressure is removed. The end product is fascinating because every person's scribbles are different, although you might think they would all look like tangled-up telephone wire. Even the voices of our scribbles manifest themselves with our unique design. In this simple, unencumbered exercise we demonstrate our diverse voices. There is an audience for everyone's expression if that expression has within it the talent it was meant to embrace—the one that comes from the heart. If we simply express our voice through words and visuals as easily as we scribble, we will share a natural and uniquely wondrous, authentic voice.

Taking the scribbling exercise a step further, we title the scribbles and, on private slips of paper, write down titles for everyone else's scribbles. There are as many different interpretations as there are scribbles. It is another reflection of the diversity of creative voices coming from the artist child within. The creative process works through each of us uniquely.

Be in wonder wherever you go and let yourself be a beginner, over and over again. Begin again… let that be a mantra.

Playing Blocks and Breaking Them

Tom is a stand-up comedian who was experiencing a dry spell. He creates a character onstage that has comical, childlike confusion. His work was getting stale, the lines fell flat, and laughs were decreasing with each show. We experimented with media other than standing up and delivering a dialogue. He found that doodling in a sketchbook right before he goes onstage freed him up to be more in character. The motion of scribbling went beyond the limited warm-up of just thinking about lines. It awakened the child that plays onstage when he is doing his delivery.

Sara was a storyteller who wanted to take her craft to a deeper, more professional level. When she practiced, she stayed stiffly in one place with limited hand gestures. I asked her to play with her story by exaggerating it and making it one of her worst deliveries ever. She varied her voice, moved around colorfully with unpredictable rhythms, made great sweeping hand motions, and basically had a lot of fun. Instead of being one of her worst deliveries, it elicited a whole new style of entertainment and fun. She used much of the exercise's results to enliven her performances.

Susan, a creative writing student, felt she had lost all the enjoyment of writing. She was having a hard time letting go of the rules of writing and what she thought she was supposed to do. She spent too much time listening to others. She did not know where to go next in the development of her characters.

I asked her to interview them or have them write her a letter. At first this suggestion perplexed her since her adult side could not comprehend how an undeveloped character could write a letter. Once the idea sank in, she lit up like a child. Each week she brought in a new letter that a character had written her. The characters had taken on such a life of their own and she could not wait to hear what they had to say next. She shared her findings with such excitement. The technique brought fun back into her writing and allowed her to be more productive.

You can do the same with any area of life or art. Figure out how imagination can give you a different viewpoint. As a visual artist, write a letter to yourself from an image ready to come into reality. If you were writing a nonfiction book about trees, Bea Silly might say, "Hey, go interview a spruce and see how you can branch out from the usual dry bark." If you were writing an article about single mothers, she might conjure up play by asking different fanciful questions like "Name a vehicle or a circus character that might describe your experience as a single mother." Bea Silly would also give you ideas for your writing from the curious, innocent, and open-minded child's point of view, a view untainted by narrow and rigid adult views.

What in your life can write you a letter to give you more insight? A symbol? A problem you are trying to solve? A creative idea trying to make itself clear? Have your next job write you a letter. Write a letter from characters in your dreams.

From Silly to Ingenuity

Ideas often seem silly just because they are new and not something the mind has yet registered as acceptable. They tarry outside the boundaries of what currently exists. This is no reason to reject them. Defying boundaries is a Muse-approved activity. The mind may be stuck in a predetermined set of boundaries.

What silly things in your life camouflage solutions and innovations? What if you had a silly brainstorm? Come up with a problem to be solved on the way to your dream and be a silly kid spurting out goofy ideas. Write them on big paper with crayons. See if something new and wonderful might come from it.

> More important than talent, strength, or knowledge is the ability to laugh at yourself and enjoy the pursuit of your dreams.
> ~ Amy Grant

MIRACLES OF LAUGHTER

During my time as a manager for hospital units, I noticed that the tension in meetings was heavy. I had to do something because my brow was getting stuck in a permanent furrow. At the beginning of the meetings I gave out squirt guns or Styrofoam balls to be thrown at judgmental comments to dissipate the tension. The laughter that ensued freed up people's minds to focus clearly on productivity. A Dr. Seuss story illustrated a problem we were having with getting people to cooperate. Hot Tamale candies were given to the staff member who showed the best motivation each week. Everyone was given, and told to peel, a banana while we got to the meat of the matter. A windup bird flapping its wings wildly without flight symbolized being all wound up and not getting anywhere. And so on. Meetings where people are awake, having fun, and releasing tension through humor strengthen team building, commitment, and motivation.

Similarly, relationships are strengthened with play (remember the saying "Those who play together, stay together"?). Laughter and being silly are harbingers of collective creativity.

PLAY

Making your approach to creativity fun can rejuvenate powers of the uninhibited freedom you had as a child. By choosing new play techniques that are not charged with painful memories or subconscious baggage that can create resistance, you can begin to express a new childlike side of you. If you are willing to let down your adult facade, you can coast into new playful action as easily as if you were sliding down a slide (unless it is a metal slide on a hot day and you are wearing shorts). Just begin to look for a new child inside you that is ready to create the ease of happiness on the outside. In the descriptions below, and in Bea Silly's Brainstorm section, find what play might be original for you to use for your dream weaving or creative passion.

Play works so well in the realm of creativity because ideas do not just appear when we are sitting down and thinking real hard. Ideas cannot resist playful movement. Play's active spontaneity is the optimal condition for creativity. That's why dance and movement are part of Bea Silly's domain. Exercise and any other kind of physical activity can also elicit ideas. The energy of exercise releases stress so the mind is free to connect to the ideas behind the tension.

The Safety of the Child

The "inner child" has been overly explored as it relates to the wounded part of us. We also have an inner child filled with joy. We can choose to use either one for our creative benefit: the child side that stubbornly refuses to let us be creative or the side that refutes the voices of the inner critic, thereby freeing us to be more creative. The child stubbornly keeps us resistant because we were hurt or are still angry. The child for us is used more effectively, keeping us stubbornly committed to our creative joy. Use of Bea Silly's techniques alchemizes the strength of our child into the conviction to participate in our creative passions no matter what.

Free Your Inner Brat

Scott was a brilliantly accomplished artist who was trying to reawaken his love of creating large mystical acrylic paintings. He was resistant to returning to his easel and did not quite know why. I prescribed various creative exercises to invite back his motivation, and each were met with a childlike frown and crossed arms. Clearly his artist child inside was not happy. He had been so caught up in the difficult responsibilities of his graphic design business that he had excluded anything fun. There was little time to enjoy the pleasures of his everyday life. Although painting is a pleasure, it takes hard work initiated by the motivation of the inner artist child. If that child has been neglected, he will not be cooperative about allowing the adult side to paint. Scott's child refused to let him paint, retaliating as if to say, "If I can't have fun, there's no way I'm letting you paint. You can't have fun either."

The next week I gave Scott the assignment of stomping around the house like an upset child, playing hooky from his work, talking back to his demanding adult voice by saying, "So what, you can't make me." I told him to rebel against and refuse a list of daily tasks I had prescribed for him. I gave him a lot of tasks so he would have a lot to rebel against. I told him to listen to what the childlike side of him wanted to do and then to indulge that child. As I made these suggestions, his face shifted to a mischievous expression. The next week he came back with a canvas filled with the beginnings of a fabulous painting. His stubborn-child side had been given an outlet and some nurturing attention. The result was a release of resistance and a reciprocation of desired artwork.

Scott also responded to the mystery of the instruction to "start your painting and see where it leads you." He was used to careful planning before starting his paintings, so a childlike sense of wonder was awakened with this instruction and he once again broke through his resistance.

If you are feeling resistant toward starting your creative projects, consider whether you have been doing enough "fun stuff" in your life. Allowing your child side to play and goof off doing anything for just fifteen minutes before you start will make it easier to get to the things the adult side wants to do.

> Play is the exultation of the possible.
> ~ Martin Buber

It is the shy, little, vulnerable artist-child side of us that is willing, or unwilling, to move forward in creativity, and the strong part of you needs to protect that child in these ways:

What if you surrounded yourself with people with whom the artist child feels comfortable? Reparent your child by providing large gestures of nurturing. Set time for yourself once a week to treat yourself to something your artist child would like. Ask your artist child, would you rather go to the art museum gift shop than the art museum? Would you rather see a frivolous movie than a serious one? Would you rather have a grilled cheese than a tofu stir-fry? As you listen to your artist child and abide by the childlike requests, you will be gifted with the power of creative energy. All of a sudden a stubborn, dormant side of you will open to the festivities of life and your imagination will become spontaneous again. When this happens, the process feels like magic.

The Wonder and Curiosity of the Child

Ask ten times with wild abandonment, "What if?" For example:

> What if people who tailgated vanished when they got too close? What if I could sing in a blues club? How about a yellows club? What if bananas flew?
> What if Jell-O molds talked?
> What if life were a bowl of eyeballs? What if I could get out of my own way?
> What if a picture could paint a thousand words?
> What if a face could launch a thousand ships? What if love were a pile of leaves?

To take the exercise to another level . . . take one of your "What if" statements and begin writing as if it were true: Life is a bowl of eyeballs and now they all need reading glasses . . . My Jell-O mold talked to me this morning about how I feel suspended with the fruit cocktail I work with . . . As soon as I get out of my way I will give myself permission to dance . . . Love is a pile of leaves and mine has little bugs in it . . . You will discover new images to paint, poetry, starts to stories, or maybe just amusement.

Mortals Who Were Inspired by Bea Silly

Listening to these mortals talk, you begin to feel the inspiration of play, dance, and laughter open you to more creativity.

> Serious people have few ideas. People with ideas are never serious. ~ Paul Valery

> People do not quit playing because they grow old.
> They grow old because they quit playing.
> ~ Oliver Wendell Holmes

A child's attitude toward everything is an artist's attitude.
~ Willa Cather

MUSE PROFILE OF BEA SILLY

Bea Silly's symbol is a playground where ideas are somersaulted into existence without effort. Bubbles passing through symbolize playful lightness and the spontaneous joy of fun movement.

RITUAL TO CALL ON BEA SILLY

Ritual materials: a balloon; pick one: crayons or finger paint or Play-Doh; cinnamon-apple Pop-Tarts; your sketchbook and/or journal; and a glass of milk.

Blow up the balloon but do not tie it. Say this sentence out loud: "Just as I release the messages that come from some strange tendency to be a rigid adult I release the hot air in this balloon. I see the gift there is in thinking and acting playfully." And then let the balloon fly through the air. (This is especially effective in a group of five or more people because as the balloons release, they sound like a bunch of kids sending defiant raspberries to the all-too-serious adult side of us.) Then, for five to fifteen minutes, play with your selected art material. When you finish, eat your toasted Pop-Tarts (or if you prefer a juicy piece of fruit perfectly in season), drink some milk (milk mustaches are encouraged), and write a statement to Bea Silly in your journal or sketchbook (preferably with a crayon). Say, "I will allow my artist-child side to have more freedom." Then say one of the affirmations listed below, clean up your mess, and take a nap (optional). Write the affirmation in your journal every day this week or write it on a card and post it where you can see it regularly before napping. Watch for bursts of playful energy and an increased willingness to do creative things in the coming week.

AFFIRMATIONS AND SMALL QUESTIONS FROM BEA

Silly

◎ I will open to my playful side and create a more balanced existence.

◎ I aspire to the freedom of being silly without worrying what people think—because being silly leads to new discoveries, lightens up my day, and is fun.

◎ Like a child, I trust that my world can be filled with wonder.

◎ Where will I find laughter today?

◎ How can I make whatever I'm doing fun today?

◎ What is one small way I can be silly in the interest of creative bliss today?

Journal Check-in

1. Quickly write or draw your Bea Silly status: What were you thinking about yourself or others when you read the chapter? Can you allow yourself to be childlike? Playful? Funny? Silly?

2. Write, draw, paint, or dance as if you were the quality of play. What would you say from the point of view of being the essence of play? Let the boundaries of your mind extend past logic and into the realm of playful imagination. The piece does not have to make sense.

3. Take a moment, relax with three let-go breaths, close your eyes, and allow your essence of Bea Silly that is inside you to come to your consciousness. Write a letter to yourself from your energy of Bea Silly. What would she (or he) suggest that you do? Write quickly and let her tell you what your own inner-artist child needs to be more cooperative and playful, and less stubborn. Let Bea Silly talk back to your critic. For each discouragement the critic says about your creative process, let Bea Silly respond with "So what, I'm doing it anyway" or "Who cares what you say." Use your inner brat to defend you rather than have a power struggle with you.

Muse Walk—Bea Silly Style

Go outside for a Muse walk. Walk with heavy feet the way you might imagine a child would walk. Feel the essence of being a child again. Skip if you would like. See the world around you through the eyes of a child. Enjoy the way your moving body feels. Feel everything that feels good about your body. Embody the feeling of having an inside joke. Let ideas playfully follow you on your walk. Feel optimism, open-mindedness, wonder, mirth. Catch ladybugs. Set them free.

Brainstorm

Getting Silly

The best way to break through the rigid bounds of being an adult that repel creativity is to begin to *talk out loud in gibberish using vocal inflections as if you were saying real words*. Do this alone, and notice if you are completely self-conscious even though you are doing it by yourself. If so, your inner critic is policing your freedom to be silly and telling you to stop because it is uncomfortable. That same discomfort will stop you from exploring creative realms. Keep doing the gibberish until you start to feel comfortable with the silliness of it, at least by yourself. Nobody is watching! Silly talk primes your child side for opening up and connecting to great new ideas.

Quick List five memories you have of being silly. What was your own special brand of silliness? Do not be concerned if you cannot think of all twenty. Your subconscious will work on it even when the list has been put away, and memories of your past silliness will then revisit you at unexpected times. If you weren't silly at all, list how you could have been silly.

Shifting into the Energy of Eagerness

Kids are often filled with eagerness for what's next. Adults can be filled with dread. Take your "I have to…" list, and change it into "I get to…". In other words, notice the shift in energy in your body when you put "I get to" in front of everything on your To-do list. The child-like spirit awakens and somehow the task is made easier. Feel the difference between these two sentences: "I have to write today" and "I GET to write today". The second one is MUCH more likely to have an "oh boy!" at the end of it and we need all the "oh boys" we can get.

STICKERS

Keep fun stickers handy to reward yourself for engaging in your creative passions. Make a weekly chart and fill it with stickers. Use them on letters to friends. To exceed your play requirements, even seal the envelopes of your bill payments with them. Somewhere inside of you is an artist child who opens up creatively anytime you do something you may have appreciated when you were a child. Stick one on your forehead.

MOVEMENT

Inspiration and ideas often come during movement, not just sitting and thinking. In fact, for kinesthetic learners and creators, most creativity happens when they are dancing, gesturing, or moving in some fashion.

Experiment with ideas by playing with them in movement. Exaggerate them as you talk about them. Playact every side, everyone involved, anyone who might see the end product. Playact as if you were the problem. Make an announcement about the product. Play with props of any kind for any kind of problem solving.

Stomp, dance, interpretive dance around the living room.

Then swing your body back and forth and let your arms swing as if they were just pinned to the shoulders. Have an "I don't care" attitude. (Do not underestimate the power of this one either.)

RAMBLINGS

In your daily journal write things a kid might, or write sideways in your journal. Scribble; comment about the world around you in kid language.

Alternatively: Explain a creative project, idea, or problem you have as if you were explaining it to a child. Explain it from a child's point of view. It is amazing what new ideas come from this childlike frame of reference.

FIELD TRIPS

(Get a permission slip signed by the adult in you.)

Spend a half to a full hour a week with the artist child; get into a childlike mentality and let him or her pick what to do.

Go to the grocery store and let your artist child pick some things to buy. Break down your rigid rules about eating in the interest of creative nourishment just once a week.

Engage in some of the creative projects that you liked to do as a child.

ART THAT'S FUN

Paint as you like and die happy.
~ Henry Miller

"Free drawing," or doodling, is an exercise to shut your brain off and let your hand move across the paper. There is a temptation to feel that a creative session is a failure if we do not create a piece of art—banish those thoughts. When you free draw there is always the possibility of a creative breakthrough. Art is a tactile exercise, and by returning to the basics, our minds will subconsciously create.

Try this exercise in the morning—before the influences of the outside world have diluted your brain and creativity. Paint: Play with paint without judging yourself. Give yourself unconditional acceptance. Title your pictures and hang them on the refrigerator. Say, "Look what I did." Have the Bodyguard sneer at anyone who doesn't absolutely love them.

HANG AROUND FUNNY FRIENDS

Find them. Play with them. Laugh with them. Keep the merry theme of life alive.

Blessed are we who can laugh at ourselves for we shall never cease to be amused.
~ Anonymous

WRITING

Play with words. Forget rules of grammar. Make up words. Play with the space on the Be silly and see what happens.

NEXT STOP IN THE GARDEN

As you walk farther into the garden, voices inside your head mock and annoy you with criticisms and belittling run-on sentences aimed at any attempt that you make toward your creativity. What they are sharing is born out of fear, not reality. You feel rattled and overworked, underappreciated and discarded. You retreat under your blanket with Ben … & Jerry.

All of a sudden, a savory soup scent leads you to the heart of the garden where there is a canopy-covered kitchen with an herb garden nearby. Conjure up the vision of the most nurturing and motherly feminine spirit that you can imagine. This is Muse Song. In her guiding presence, you feel encouraged, taken care of, watched over, and totally appreciated for the gift of who you are. You may know or have known someone like her, or you may want to make a composite of several people from your past who nurtured and/or encouraged you. You may also want to mobilize these same powers inside of yourself and spend some valuable nurturing energy on yourself … your creativity will flourish. Muse Song is the heart of the garden, and walking through the sheltering aroma of her kitchen endows you with her presence from here forward.

Muse Song says, "You are a magnificent creative spirit and trust that what you create from your heart will bless the world. Your true self is beautiful, and we want you to share it."

Muse Song

MUSE SONG:
MUSE OF NURTURING, ENCOURAGEMENT, AND GOOD COMPANY

A friend is someone who knows the song in your heart and can sing it back to you when you have forgotten the words.
~ Unknown

SUMMON MUSE SONG TO

- Discover how self-love is a conduit for flourishing creative expression.
- Shift your self-talk in order to empower your creativity, not squash it.
- Prompt you to choose people who believe in your creative potential and support your efforts.

⊚ Explore the positive effects sharing and service has on your creativity.

Bottom Line

Liking who we are is vital for creativity. If we don't, why would we think we have something worth sharing with others? When we treat ourselves like precious instruments of creativity, the result is prolific creative output. Undoing our negative inner talk is vital to move past thinking what does not serve us and to our creative and spiritual growth. Surround yourself with people who inspire and support you. Support others. Stand for a cause, or, make a cause for celebration.

The Selection of Muse Song

The next Modern Day Muse manifestation embodies one of the most powerful influences of creative rebirth: self-love or at the very least, self-like. Mortals seemed to be sadly lacking in this area, a perplexing condition to the Muses, who have another book out entitled *Self-Pamper Profusely Without Apology*. They thought, "How can a precious instrument of creative expression operate with smooth excellence if it is not properly maintained with praise, pampering, and pleasurably positive experiences?" So they vowed to change the mortal tune of self-badgering to a song of self-praise. They materialized a Muse named Muse Song, whose melodic compassion can soothe the savage beast that sometimes resides in the mortal's own mind. She inspires harmony within us, and in our relationships with others.

Your Muse Song Energy

The energy Muse Song emits is about care and nurturing. This energy has been considered important enough to be "Muse-worthy" because the art of self-nourishment has a profound effect on mortals' creative productivity.

Steps of the Self-Kindness Accords

1. Become Aware of Your Self-Talk

Self-talk is often either based on trust or on fear. The difference is clear. Fear will convince us not to take steps that result in our self-expansion. Trust will encourage us to follow our dreams, feel fear as an affirmation of growth, and stay true to the paths that are making themselves known according to our unique beauty.

We can't always be positive; the negativity bias comes with the territory of being human. If we are curious about our thinking, normalize the parts that feel critical, but employ more helpful self-talk, we won't be using a lot of energy trying to change things; we can use it to think up new ideas. One of the keys is repetition.

2. Implement Awareness

Start listening to what you are telling yourself as if you were an observer of your own thoughts.

Maintain the practice with patience and although you will never eliminate the inner critic, you may soften its effect on you. But patience is key. Muse Song stresses the following fine point: If you do not have patience with the process, it can backfire on you and scar your intention. Allow all your thoughts to be there; give more attention to the ones that serve you.

Another key is not to judge yourself for judging yourself. In other words, stay compassionate even when those voices come up, breathe a sigh of acknowledgment, and accept that your self-judgment as part of being human. The struggle then is over, and the inner critic is more likely to stop its attacks because it's not having fun anymore.

3. Self-Encouragement and Good Witches

In her book *The Captive Muse*, Susan Kolodny explains that almost every individual who ventures into the creative realm is afflicted with voices that try to discourage him or her. Successful artists, poets, writers, and expressers of creative passions replace the critical, chiding, or discouraging voices with voices that applaud, praise, and encourage. We have that choice. The benevolent new voices come from mentors, teachers, or other guides from the creative individual's past or present. And if encouraging voices cannot be recalled, successful artists invent them. Creating a new reassuring voice to replace the inner critic will make the difference between quitting and triumphing.

The Self-Nurturing Deal

Muse Song is delighted to share this stunning secret creativity with you. It is a win-win thing. Here it is: You start doing nice things for yourself, and the self that is responsible for creative expression begins to poke itself out of hiding and begins to create. Start by asking what it would look and feel like to be nurturing to yourself.

Reverse Logic

Sometimes, nurturing means stopping the work for a while, giving yourself a break, contacting Lull. Other times, a true sense of safety and nurturing comes from getting some of the grunt work out of the way with Marge. This is how Marge works with Muse Song:

First thing in the morning, instead of making a long to do list, pick a "north star" for the day. Choose something difficult but significant to your creative journey and get it done. The rest of the day, you will feel fulfilled and that's one of the most nurturing things you can do. Foil any resistance for focusing just on the first thirty seconds of doing it, knowing that you are taking care of yourself in a Muse Song manner.

The People Around You: Who Are They and What Are They Doing There?

Surround yourself with only people who are going to lift you higher.
~ Oprah Winfrey

When we come up with a good idea, we often have an immediate impulse to want to share it with anyone around. Muse Song advises caution in these circumstances. Share your delicate creative ideas only with people you consider safe. Not everyone is. If a mate or a parent discourages your creativity . . . keep your ideas to yourself or to your chosen circle of sincere supporters at least until its firmly set in your confidence. Charles Brower noted, "A new idea is delicate. It can be killed by a sneer or a yawn; it can be stabbed to death by a joke or worried to death by a frown on the right person's brow." Consult the Bodyguard and employ Muse Song with some nurturing words.

Develop an inner circle of your own creative angels: people who support, believe in, and encourage you. If you don't have these people, find them by taking classes or joining creative support groups and notice which people you gravitate toward. Wake up when you spot people who are encouraging to you and make an effort to bring them into your inner circle. Have a mutual admiration club. Find people who are easy for you to encourage and praise, as well.

Insert Here: A Moment of Pondering About People Who Stimulate Your Creativity

When you have a trusted group of creative angels, bounce your ideas off them. I sometimes think I am the only one who can do my creative work, and I am pleasantly surprised when I hear people's wonderful new slants on my projects. Some of their feedback can move what I am doing to a richer, more accessible level. We are creative conduits, each and every one of us, and the source that provides inspiration is greater than us all. The more we contribute to each other, the greater we become ourselves.

Mortals Who Were Inspired by Muse Song

As you walk through this part of the garden, once again you hear echoes of mortals who validate the inspirations of Muses. This time you begin to understand the importance of nurturing yourself for the creative process.

> Keep away from people who belittle your ambitions. Small people always do that, but the really great make you feel that you, too, can become great.
> ~ Mark Twain

> The future belongs to those who believe in the beauty of their dreams.
> ~ Eleanor Roosevelt

> Remember, you have been criticizing yourself for years and it hasn't worked. Try approving of yourself and see what happens. ~ Louise Hay

> When I'm inspired, I get excited because I can't wait to see what I'll come up with next.
> ~ Dolly Parton

Muse Profile of Muse Song

SYMBOL

Muse Song's symbol is two teacups, inviting the feeling of being nurtured in the company of encouraging friends. Both are in harmony with creative expansion.

HOBBIES

Always having a cup of soothing tea ready, hanging art on refrigerators, writing notes of praise, consulting on the art of luxuriating baths, channeling of exercise and nutrition information, knitting, and karaoke singing.

RATE YOURSELF ON MUSE SONG'S METER FOR NURTURING

| Self-flagellation is your favorite past-time, this is a no-frills life for you; you get sick a lot | You berate yourself every day but Sunday; you had a massage once in '89; you work too much | You tell yourself you are good at what you do only if it makes you money | You like the way you treat others and you take yourself to movies twice a month | You get massages once a month, you practice affirmations; you feel pretty good about yourself | Your healthy self-love results in great feats of creativity for yourself and others |

MUSE SONG AFFIRMATIONS AND SMALL QUESTIONS

◉ I am gentle with myself at least 30% of the time.

◉ What does being kind and gentle to myself LOOK and FEEL like?

◉ I choose to associate with people who genuinely support and encourage my creativity.

◉ I am a precious instrument of creativity so I am conscientious about taking care of needs, especially the ones relating to doing my best at thinking and acting creatively.

◉ Can't wait to see what I have to express creatively.

◉ What's one small way I can be kind in this moment?

And there ya go. Muse Song is present with you.

Journal Check-in

1. Quickly write or draw where you are with Muse Song. Begin with: In the Self-Kindness realm I . . . What do you do well in the Muse Song realm?

2. Look at the quotes by mortals who were inspired by Muse Song throughout the chapter. Pick one or more and continue the essence of the quote in your own words or speed-write how the quote applies to you.

3. Relax, get comfortable, add some extra pillows, and notice the nurturing nature of your breath. Move into a receptive mode and allow yourself to fully receive the next inhale as if it were a gift of life. Let it go as if you were floating down a river of nurturing golden light - no effort, floating on all that supports who you are. Embody Muse Song's compassion and nurturing as your own. When you are ready, write a letter from Muse Song to yourself. Let her give you suggestions about taking care of yourself, your selection of friends, support with your journey, and pampering yourself.

Muse Walk—Muse Song Style

Take a walk and let yourself fully receive the pleasure and solitude of a nurturing journey. Let your body take on the feeling of being loved and appreciated. Feel a sense of inner encouragement and notice what changes occur in your posture or in your stride. Take in the beauty around you as if it were a gift created especially for you. Ask yourself, "What in this moment feels nurturing?"

Muse Song Suggestions

- Make a list of people who you feel good around, consider getting together more often.

- Buy yourself a magazine subscription, follow a blog, or listen to podcasts that encourage your art, music, writing, dance, photography, crafting, etc.

- Leave encouraging notes for yourself in drawers, pockets, cabinets, on dog collars.

- Collect compliments and keep them where you can see them or have a book of compliments . . . seriously, do it.

- Breathe in the power of compliments, feel their goodness in your body's energy and if it's hard for you to accept them, accept them just 5% more than you usually do. Compliments fuel the confidence that creative people need.

- Engage in altruism to encourage your creative unveiling and self-discovery.

- Take moments every now and then to just breathe with nurturing your mind and body as the only purpose.

CREDIT REPORTS AND POWER TOOLS

Many of my clients seek creativity coaching because they feel they are not moving fast enough toward their creative goals. When they do the following exercise, the energy and insight they receive from it propels them forward. Try it yourself. It seems so obvious but it is so overlooked.

Make a list of what you have already accomplished regarding your creative goal. List everything and do not minimize anything. Often what you see is the evidence that you are doing more than you thought you were doing. Seeing some groundwork motivates more and just plain feels good. Ask yourself these questions:

Where did I get it right?
What's working?
What else might work?
What am I glad I did?

How would it feel to believe that the things I have done today are enough?

When we stretch wide open the moment that we give ourselves credit, we benefit energetically and creatively.

THE PEOPLE AROUND YOU: WHO ARE THEY AND WHY ARE THEY THERE?

Who is your inner circle of friends? Whom do you need to keep on the outside of the circle?

Draw a circle in your sketchbook so you have a visual for yourself to see mentally as you proceed in your creative process. Include on the inside people who are there . . .

For self-esteem, support, catalysts of ideas;

Who in your life has encouraged you in the past and currently does in the present?

Who is taking up a lot of your time at your expense?

Place on the outside . . . people you love but need to be careful of because they don't yet understand your creativity;

People you simply need to steer clear of.

Do you need to draw boundaries with anyone or anything, and if so, who, what, and how? Whom do you choose to share your creative work and secrets with?

YOUR PERSONAL MUSES

What real, fictional, historical, or contemporary figures positively influence you? Often, keeping their names where you can see them frequently will instill in you the traits you so admire in them. Take a moment now and scribe a list on a piece of paper separate from your journal. Write it neatly, calligraphically, or type it and place it on the front of your journal or in a picture frame where you can see it.

Frugal Extravagance

Here is a list of inexpensive things you could buy yourself. Endow each with a little imagination and let the special powers make your day more fun. A little spell of magic in the creative realm goes a long way to give you a feeling of being special and staying in the moment:

- A special washcloth: Endow it with the power to wash away your negativity. One big, new special towel: a color different from all the others that you would buy if it didn't clash with your bathroom. Endow it with the power to wrap you in a loving embrace that attracts good people into your life.

- Although a pint of raspberries may seem expensive, comparatively speaking, for one's pampering pleasure, it's cheap. Indulge your senses with the taste of each one. Let each be a wild explosive pill of creative exuberance.

- Buy a soft, fuzzy rug to place under your desk so you can take your shoes off and have a pampered feeling. In the winter, place a heating pad under your feet.

- During your creative times, wear special clothes filled with creativity. Why wear old clothes just in case you get messy? Even for painters: Get fun new clothes meant just to make your creative time more special. Let them take on more character with each mess you make. Or, get a great new apron you can mess up. Even if you are in a non-messy craft, do the same.

A Token of My Inspiration

Creative people sometimes have a totem that brings them more inspiration. Find a picture, statue, button, memorabilia, quote, novel art project, or whatever that will trigger a positive belief and post it, wear it, or string it from your ceiling. Find a little icon of creativity to place on your desk and endow it with creative power.

DEDICATIONS

When engaging in your creative work, dedicate it to someone important to you. This will infuse the process with a power that goes beyond you. You do not even need to tell whoever it is about the dedication. Just knowing you have made the dedication will bring out a sacred quality in your approach to your creativity. Do it for each session and for the finished product.

NEXT STOP IN THE GARDEN

Across the garden path are strewn waded-up pieces of paper, paint spills, rejected drawings, and an occasional banana peel. You hear laughter close by and come to a clearing with a big table filled with media for art, music, and all other kinds of creative expression. An impish character invites you over and asks you to experiment with the media on the table.

"Allow the stumble of serendipity and the discoveries that come with imperfections, to happen. In mistakes," she says, "you discover the beauty of unplanned genius and surrender the affliction of control."

You decide to comply, and you gravitate toward your favorite section of art, music, dance, writing, or simply feeling creative. You hesitate because you are a little afraid of doing something that doesn't look good or sound good, or you are afraid of looking like a fool. Spills convinces you to begin anyway, because it is the process, not the product, that is filled with wondrous joy. It is the fool, not the image-obsessed mortal, who triumphs by risking his or her appearance to live a deeper, more meaningful life.

SPILLS:
MUSE OF PRACTICE, PROCESS AND IMPERFECTION

"He who hesitates because he feels inferior is being surpassed by he who is busy making mistakes and becoming superior."
~ Henry Link

SUMMON SPILLS WHEN:

◎ You are avoiding the creative process due to:
   Fear of not being good enough
   Fear of failure
   Fear of change
   Overwhelm
   Not knowing where to begin
   Immobilization
   Unrealistic expectations (there is an EPIDEMIC of unrealistic expectations).

◎ You seem to focus on details far too long; your progress is confined because you spend too much time reworking things to make them perfect, which they never seem to be.

Bottom Line

Both life and creativity are processes to experience, not to judge. Spills manifests her energy as the inner part of us that relishes the discoveries that take place in our imperfect approach to the world. We evolve only when we participate, not when we sit on the sidelines fearing inadequacy. And the more we act, the more wisdom, confidence, and excellence we receive. Trusting the process leads to peace and contentment. Release impatience. Dive in; you will rise to the top. Instead of focusing on the final product, ask yourself how you are becoming a better person by immersing in this divine process.

Decide to align your process with your choice of glorious qualities versus qualities that sneak in when we default to old patterns. Choose a sense of lightness, joy, mirth, mischievousness, irreverence, openness, or wonder. Lose the popular defaults of rigidity, pressure, judgment, torment, and hurry.

And if you should strive for perfection in a way that makes you feel like a failure when you don't meet unreasonable expectations and feel your worth is dependent on doing things perfectly:

1. Have compassion for having this misguided belief system you've bought into
2. Forgive yourself
3. Recalibrate your expectations to "close enough" from "impossible"
4. Notice all the wonderful things you are that you've overlooked, even if it's just 5%

The Selection of Spills

Spills came into being purely by mistake. The Muses were playing with the attributes they thought that the next Muse should embody. They kept saying things they really didn't mean to say, but which actually seemed clever anyway. They drew blueprints with a lot of fumbles, yet each blunder led to an insight that led to a consideration of something new, which made them laugh about the serendipity of ideas, which made the process uncommon, which gave them the next Muse. "Mistakes! That's it. Oops, no, that's not it," one of them said, then corrected herself. She had said that by mistake. Here's what was important: they were engaged in the process and not just thinking, avoiding, and fearing it. The result: discovery.

The serendipity of mistakes is part of the magic of the creative process. Within the process, spills, mistakes, and imperfections are a method of discovery. So Spills was created. Since she's on the uncoordinated side of things, they thought making her an imp would be endearing.

Your Spills Energy

*A man of genius makes no mistakes.
His errors are volitional and are the portals of discovery. ~
James Joyce*

The word spills implies "Oops, didn't mean to do that." But when seen through the lens of discovery, spills or mistakes become agents of possibility. Spills imparts to mortals the wisdom of loving the process. She emphasizes the importance of releasing preconceptions about, and attachments to, the end result. Practice and patience allow awkwardness to spill into grace.

Spills also advocates the release of perfectionism. She knows that expecting mistakes and inadequacies makes creative genius possible. Expecting instant adequacy or perfection is antithetical to the creative process. Discovery cannot happen without trial and error. Excellence cannot happen without practice. You CAN begin even if at the beginning of a process you don't have all the information, skills, knowledge, tools and materials. The beauty is in discovering, through the creative process, what direction to take next. Unfortunately, an entire continent of mortals is frozen in perfection's paralysis. Spills' work is not easy and she does not expect it to be. Spills is always in the present moment and believes that the process is a constant state of unfolding discoveries. The results of our efforts may not be great at the beginning, but with practice they will bring a beautiful blossoming of our evolving abilities.

All efforts have merit in the unfolding of our beauty. None are meaningless, none are wasted.

The only way to traverse your creative path incorrectly is not to traverse it at all. Spills says, "Hey, mortal, don't have any judgment about what you do. There is no good or bad ... just curiosity and excitement for all the surprises the process brings. All of your attempts and actions are the practice you need in order to be the best mortal possible. Being engaged in the process makes the deepening of your existence possible. The refusal to participate because of your fear of imperfection and inadequacy is the stunting of your spiritual excellence. Peace of mind and creative freedom come with the release of perfection."

> Sometimes we strive so hard for perfection
> that we forget that imperfection is happiness.
> ~ Karen Nave

The creative process is nonlinear. We do not traverse a straight line to our dreams but, instead, encounter many surprises and new directions. Spills says, "Hey, mortal [she says that a lot], be open to where the process takes you and stay the course that's true to yourself. Striving for a perfect series of results according to calculated actions, and expecting a rigid set of images with no room for variation, is the way of damaging control. Control is not cool. It is used when you don't trust the process. If you fiddle with the process because you are rigid about what your dream must look like, you miss the signs that lead to a more penetrating dream, the one most suited to you. And you miss out on the joy of a process that is filled with the remarkable gifts of your unfolding self." Spills is fairly articulate despite being an imp and all.

Allen Ginsberg talks about his submission to letting go of control. "I really don't know what I'm doing when I sit down to write. I figure it out as I go along. I see the writing is interesting if there are a lot of awkward poetic ideas made up by accident in the course of rapid notation of thoughts. It's usually a subject I've wondered about before, so it's a matter of transcription in visual shorthand of whatever is on my mind, plus spontaneous improvisation and excitement when I realize I'm suddenly talking about something I never did before."

Pablo Picasso said, "To know what you're going to draw, you have to begin drawing."

Countless successful artists from every area of expression will tell you it was the process that brought them the most happiness, not the final product.

Mass media and the school system have contributed to the epidemic of people wanting to look and perform only perfectly. In school we are often judged and graded according to a system of rigid acceptability. Deviations and novel expressions are discouraged, conforming is encouraged. Imperfection is shamed and the unrealistic goal of perfection is promoted and equated with worth and desirability. Imperfect acts, statements, and especially creative expressions are discouraged.

The media bombards us with airbrushed perfection and individuals who convey perfection only through their looks.

Perfection Paralysis

"This needs to be done just perfectly or not at all." Good luck. Perfectionists can be people who strain compulsively and unremittingly toward impossible goals and who measure their worth entirely in terms of productivity and accomplishment. Many people stop themselves from living deeply because they fear looking inadequate or they are impatient with how long it takes to be "good" at something. They live with careful restraint and constipated happiness. It is a sad struggle . . . but there IS help. You probably know if you are one of them, because you are chronically frustrated with, or fearful of, the creative process. See if any of these sound familiar to you:

- You keep redoing your work over and over and over and over and over, and you are still not satisfied with it.
- You do not begin your creative passion at all for fear of failure or looking inadequate.
- Your mind goes blank at the request or intention to begin anything requiring creativity.
- You put yourself under so much pressure to perform perfectly that you block doing anything at all.

- You do not enjoy any part of the creative process because it is a constant reminder of how inadequate you are.

- Your expectations are unrealistic. Starting seems overwhelming, so you avoid it completely.

- You think excellent results should happen immediately, and if they don't, you give up. You underestimate the amount of practice it takes to begin to master a creative passion, and you label yourself inadequate way before you've given yourself a chance to flower.

- You insist on doing all the work yourself even when it would make sense to request help from others to ensure your success. You fear that others cannot perform up to your standards.

If you have perfection paralysis, you are not alone. Currently an epidemic, it is responsible for much of life's disillusionment. When you are striving for perfection, your happiness is dependent upon unrealistic goals. Pointless to galactic proportions! Spills directs you through a passage that leads to creative enjoyment. Follow the steps she discovered in her enlightenment of mortals:

- Breathe, and enjoy the process of breathing. Know that releasing the torment of perfectionist thoughts will take practice. Don't expect to be perfect at accepting imperfection. (This may sound funny, but a perfectionist trying to kick the habit will place just as high expectations on herself to do that as anything else.)

- One of the most successful approaches we have in Kaizen-Muse Creativity Coaching is lowering expectations at the beginning. Give yourself permission not only to put less pressure on yourself, but give yourself permission to do things badly at first. Make it fun. Try approaching the beginning or process of your next project with small and crappy in mind and notice the liberation and willingness to begin that you feel.

- Step into the process of life and of your creative passion. Exercise acceptance with the knowledge that with practice you will get better at anything. It's a universal law.

- Practice compassion with yourself and others. When thoughts of impatience arise because something seems imperfect, breathe again. Label the thought an "irrational judgment". Embody an air of acceptance even if initially it feels awkward and unreal. You are breaking patterns that are difficult to break because they are old, not because they are right.

- Practice your creative passion without judgment. If judgment arises, breathe and release the judgment with your exhale. Breathe in the present moment and allow yourself the luxury of being a student.

- Have patience: Accept your initial awkwardness with the same compassion that you would accept a small child's learning something new. If you are impatient even with small children, take a step back and pay attention to your unrealistic expectations.

- Have patience with practice.

- And practice patience patiently.

- Relax and let the magic of surrendering to the creative process with grace and acceptance create YOU as a better person. Just be you and know it's all perfect if you don't judge it.

> I have not failed. I've just found ten thousand ways that won't work.
> ~ Thomas Alva Edison

Thomas Edison tried ten thousand different materials before finding one that was suitable to serve as a lightbulb filament. We need to set up a system where risk is rewarded. One where we recognize that failure helps us to increase our creativity. Nothing risked is nothing gained.

THE COMPETENCE ADDICTION

Another crinkle in creative growth is the competence addiction—our ego's addiction to competence. We may become attached to skill in one area of our work in order to avoid the discomfort of returning to beginner status in some area waiting to delight us. We may have overidentified with our current limited job description and felt insecure and stubborn about starting something new. We must be willing to be a beginner over and over again in order to live a full life. Otherwise, we will be stuck in a restricted realm of existence. Sometimes we are stuck in the competence predicament without realizing what has happened. If you notice a sense of disillusionment that you cannot seem to put your finger on, consider whether you are willing to venture into something that can widen the range of your existence.

Willingness to be a beginner is rewarded with the expansion and amazement of how much more life continues to give. Profound opportunities dawn regularly.

When you surrender to the acceptance of any result that your participation delivers, you move from judgment to wonder. The most enlightened beings approach life always as students, open to learning something new about themselves or about their craft. They work not toward one end, but into the bliss of the moment.

Another View of Perfectionism

> Normal perfectionists are described as individuals who "derive a very real sense of pleasure from the labors of a painstaking effort," while neurotic perfectionists are those "unable to feel satisfaction because in their own eyes they never seem to do things good enough to warrant that feeling."
> ~ Wayne D. Parker and Karen K. Adkins

Conversely, the quest for perfection has also hurtled many people into new levels of success when they know when to stop. Healthy perfectionism is actually defined as going for excellence, not perfection. It means staying with a project or an idea for a reasonable amount of time in order to get the most excellent result and then saying "close enough!". We can spend an infinity trying to improve works of creativity because, for the most part, all works are works-in-progress.

Mortals Who Were Inspired by Spills

You hear the echoes of more mortals. Sometime what they say can make clear the importance of letting go of the pressure to be perfect.

"Remember the two benefits of failure. First, if you do fail, you learn what doesn't work; and second, the failure gives you the opportunity to try a new approach."
~ Roger Von Oech

Remember that fear always lurks behind perfectionism. Confronting your fears and allowing yourself the right to be human can, paradoxically, make you a far happier and more productive person.
~ David M. Burns

Some mistakes are too much fun to only make once. ~ Anonymous

If you can't make a mistake, you can't make anything. ~ Marva Collins

The higher up you go, the more mistakes you are allowed. Right at the top, if you make enough of them, it's considered to be your style. ~ Fred Astaire

What a wonderful life I've had!
I only wish I'd realized it sooner.
~ Colette

Muse Profile of Spills

Symbol

Spills' symbol is a spill of discovery.

HOBBIES

Pushing things over, deliberate accidents, exercising awe, espousing patience, lobbying for experimentation in the face of fear, biting bullets, and being tickled at the ingenuity that comes from releasing the fear of being i^mper_fecT. Good humor during failed attempts.

The greatest mistake a man can make is to be afraid of making one.
~ Elbert Hubbard

AFFIRMATIONS AND SMALL QUESTIONS FROM SPILLS

- What would it feel like if I were free from the need to be perfect?
- I get to be imperfect in the creative process – imperfection can become a style.
- I am evolving into someone I love for who I am, not for what I do.
- What would it feel like to truly enjoy the process?
- I am willing to be a beginner at my craft. I am getting better and better with regular practice.
- When I find myself working too hard to reach my unrealistic expectations, I will just stop and say "Close enough!"

And there you go. Spills is with you.

JOURNAL CHECK-IN

1. Take out your journal. Write or draw about your Spills status. What thoughts did the chapter bring up for you? Start with one of these unfinished sentences: Giving myself permission to do things imperfectly… or I am jumping right into the process by… I shall season my process with…

2. For the next five minutes imagine you are a "mistake." Write, draw, dance, or paint as a mistake would. See if there are any discoveries. What are your feelings in the process? Is it easy to create from this point of view?

3. Relax. Take some deep let-go breaths and embody your own Spills energy. When you are ready write yourself a letter from her, let her comment and encourage you in areas of perfectionism, practice, and being in the process. Let her counter what your inner critic said and be an advocate for your progress.

Permission To Be Imperfect

Purposely perform below your standards in any creative activity just to experience the "permission to be imperfect". Title it when you are finished. Notice how it felt. If it was difficult, write an affirmation to help advance you to a more process-oriented place.

Muse Walk—Spills Style

Take a walk simply to walk. Have no destination in mind and notice what that feels like. Allow yourself to wander off your usual path. What thoughts does it bring up? Feel the breeze created by your walking wash across your face. Feel your feet caress the earth. Match the rhythm of your breathing to the rhythm of your walking. Look for different colors. Focus only on reds, then greens, then blues. Listen for every sound you can hear. Then listen for only one. Feel yourself perfectly imperfect and let that relax you. Ask: What does feeling no pressure at all in the creative process feel like? What does trusting the process feel like? How can I reframe how imperfect I am so that I feel its gift?

Breathing

Breathing is under both automatic and voluntary control. The act, feel, and art of breathing are overlooked by many of us as some of life's most powerful and pleasurable processes. The creative importance of breathing, as far as Spills goes, is in using the pleasure of breathing to open our awareness to other enjoyable processes. As we learn to find pleasure in something as natural and available as the breath, our pleasure awareness will begin to apply to other areas of our lives. As we practice focusing on the pleasure of an automatic process such as breathing on a conscious level over and over, the pleasure itself can become automatic. Then, the state of contentment and relaxation will be as effortless as breathing. At this point, we are more able to engage in creative passions.

When you breathe as a conduit for the creative process, it serves as a release for fear that comes up around performing perfectly. Focusing on the breath joins us with the present moment. In the pure mindfulness of this very moment, there is no fear. The breath is a remedy for many of the reasons the mind is not present. In the creative process it can energize the magnetism of our inspirations.

Take a moment and return to the breath. Follow its process and notice how the simple shift of focus from thought to the process of breathing relaxes mind and body. Inspiration and joy are now more accessible.

A Grounding Breath

The following breath exercise brings alive appreciation of breathing. It relieves anxiety and returns our focus to the eternal flow of the here and now.

- Inhale halfway and hold for four seconds.
- Inhale again and hold for four seconds.
- Exhale halfway and hold for four seconds.
- Exhale to a natural stopping point and hold for four seconds.
- One more time, exhale, squeezing the air out as the abdomen pushes in and hold for eight seconds.
- Inhale halfway and hold for four seconds.
- Let go of the control of the breath and stay with the feeling of the breath's unrestricted flow for the next two cycles of inhale and exhale.
- Repeat twice.

This breathing exercise is a metaphor for the flow of the creative process: taking an inspiration, holding it, bringing more to the inspiration and holding it, exhaling as it is expressed, and stopping and exhaling again, and again letting go of the idea. Then letting go of control and surrendering to the sweet, unobstructed flow of both breathing and creativity.

Making Practice Fun

If you dread practicing, use some Muse techniques to make it more enticing. See some of Albert's ideas. Use his associative word triggers during your practice for new ideas. Imagine you are practicing in front of different audiences. Dress up the environment. Warm up to practicing by playing. Talk to yourself as if you were talking to a TV audience about what you need to practice, and how. Practice with friends. Play music, burn incense, wear a special fun outfit that is just for practicing. Reward yourself for practicing. Just practice. Experiment with attaching feelings of play, mischievousness, zaniness, and wild abandon to your process.

Quick Tips and Musings

- Change your standards to sixty percent (if you're a perfectionist performing at 150%, considering lowering them to 145%). Notice relaxation set in as you do. (Experiment with 90%!)

- Let go of unrealistic expectations and decide to allow the process to be pressure-free and enjoyable.

- Write a list of five things you would do if you could do them perfectly. Take note whether you could do any part of anything on the list just to experience the process. Take note if you are avoiding something because you want to be instantly good at it. If you gave yourself one year to be "good" at it just for the fun of it, would you change your mind about trying it?

- Spend time with someone engaged in his/her craft who is not a perfectionist. It is SO freeing!

- When you finish something and you are critical of it, check to see if your criticism is realistic. Figure out what you learned from it and what part you do like; be reasonable and compassionate about what you don't like. You can like some of it and not all of it… and still accept it.

- Develop compassion for yourself and others. Compassion happens quicker through trial and error. Find people who are compassionate toward you. Compassion as described by Kristin Neff consists of 1) Understanding you're not alone 2) Mindfulness 3) Self-Kindness.

- Be willing to look like a beginner in order to become an expert. Understand that this is common sense.

- Examine how perfectionism affects your ability to experience all of your feelings, including inadequacy, guilt, shame, anger, inferiority, jealousy, and envy. Experiencing all your feelings can move you more deeply into creativity. Allowing the imperfection feelings to surface also gives permission to joy.

- Read *Bird by Bird* by Anne Lamott, for perfection breakthrough strategies.

- Read *Drawing on the Right Side of the Brain* by Betty Edwards.

- Make up a book (or story or poem) called *Drawing on the Wrong Side of The Bird*.

SPILLS SPEAKS SOME MORE

1. If you do something over and over, trying to get it perfect, set a time limit and stop. Come back to it later, but at one point know what you have done is enough and then let go of it. Generally, we have a hard time stopping when we are too attached to the end result. Know that there is a time to release and move on.

2. Release your need for you, or your work, to be accepted. It is a wonderfully freeing feeling to give yourself a designated work period, then to set free your completed result. This makes rejection or criticism unimportant since you have done your best during the process and have now decided to be

unattached to what happens. If the results meet with success, the process again is the most important part.

3. Be aware if you spend a lot of time on details that are unimportant or that you can return to once the bulk of work is done. Focusing on unimportant aspects of your project is usually an avoidance strategy. You may do it to avoid harder work, responsibility, or the discomfort of forging into the unknown. Explore these possibilities and make sure you are prioritizing and focusing on what is most important to the project's process. If you feel you are losing sight of what is significant, a trusted opinion from someone safe, whom you respect, can be helpful.

Next Stop in the Garden

You are starry-eyed from what you have seen so far in the garden. You feel inspired to share more of yourself with the world, whether it is through art or writing, or the splendid unique way you express yourself daily. You know the Bodyguard is there to protect you, but you still feel constricted, vulnerable, and shy. You wonder how people get up the courage to be creative, or more authentic. How are they so bold to share their projects? The inner critic taunts you by saying that your desire to be creative is not worth the risk.

The trees restlessly wave about because a Muse of great authenticity is about to assist you.

The garden is alive with her energy, her ability to seize the moment and set it on fire with unbridled enthusiasm. She is alive with the desire to share her energy. She cannot wait to help you impart upon the world your unique way of being and your creative expression: art, writing, dance performance, letter writing, photography, music, just being you. She will help you move forward with confidence, courage, and genuine expression.

Her most ardent messages:
"Be yourself!"
and
"Share yourself with the world without hesitation."

AUDACITY:
MUSE OF COURAGE AND UNINHIBITED UNIQUENESS

"My darling girl, when are you going to realize that being normal is not necessarily a virtue? It rather denotes a lack of courage!" ~ Alice Hoffman

SUMMON AUDACITY WHEN:

- You need to boldly move beyond the insecurities you have about creatively sharing yourself. You want confidence and courage to proceed with your creative dream.
- You want to be yourself, but feel inhibited by, or at the mercy of, what other people think of you. You also feel at the mercy of your own excessive self-criticism.
- You need to accept and use your own power as an individual.

Bottom Line

As mortals who are given creative propensities (ALL OF US), we have the ability to manifest our personal authenticity and unique form of creative brilliance. Through our willingness to share our originality, we share with the world the beauty, insight, and ingenuity we were born with. We must share with audacious courage, believing that, as we do, we make a sweeping statement that can change the world around us.

The Selection of Audacity

It took little deliberation for the Muses to come up with this modern equivalent. Trying to stay nonjudgmental, the Muses kept correcting themselves when they referred to mortals as "those wimps". "Oops, we mean mortals," they would correct themselves time after time. Muses are compassionate beings, but they often err on the side of being a little too brazen. They just cannot believe how many mortals sell out their creative brilliance because they are afraid of what other mortals might think.

Because look, here is the reality—mortals think judgmental thoughts toward another mortal's creative expression substantially less often than imagined. If another mortal does think something judgmental, that thought process usually takes up, mmm, maybe thirty seconds AT THE MOST. Think about it—self-conscious mortals hold back their destined creative exaltation, often for their entire lives, because they fear a thirty-second judgment from other mortals who don't deserve that much power in the first place. Or mortals refuse to engage in their creativity because a misguided mortal from the past WAS judgmental and given too much power for those judgments. These timid mortals just need a little more self-compassionate moxie, a little more ... audacity. And when the Muses reached that conclusion, Aha-phrodite said, "Yes ... audacity is exactly what they need, so let's make 'Audacity' a Muse." The others concurred, unanimously streaked across a football field (at dawn, so no one was there).

Your Audacity Energy

Power is the ability not to have to please.
~ Elizabeth Janeway

The word "audacity" is a synonym for boldness, daring, and courage. Other synonyms include grit, guts, and appropriately—patience. The Muse Audacity is here to inspire these qualities in order to endow mortals with the courage they need to be creatively liberated, and to be themselves without explanation or apology.

Audacity wants mortals to know that being genuine frees others who need a beacon to guide them. Then we will have more authentic mortals running around, and fewer cranky, confused, and painfully shy ones.

Audacity brings to us a knowing that reflects a strong sense of certainty that comes with intuition. When we listen to the wisdom of intuition conveyed to us from our inner resources, we find that listening to ourselves, rather than to others, is the most important way to know and trust the truth of who we are. Likewise, we will know how to share this truth in whatever way we are inspired to do so. Intimately knowing and trusting ourselves is a form of overcoming barriers created by thinking someone else has to approve of us or of our creative work. Our consequent power dwarfs the effect of opinions, criticism, or negativity.

We learn to know ourselves by experience, awareness, and acting according to what we feel is right in the moment and then weighing the consequences of our actions from an objective standpoint. Success in the form we visualize is not guaranteed. Constant success is in fact contraindicated in both creativity and the growth of an individual. So much more insight and depth of living arise, so many more ideas are discovered, from the balance of successes and failures. If the decisions from our own wisdom result in success, we feel more confident. If they meet with failure but we remain tenacious, focused, and committed to a path true to ourselves, our self-respect grows. Self-respect results in personal freedom and confidence. Steadfastly following our own wisdom in the realm of creativity, to the degree that we can without expert opinions, is a win-win confidence builder.

What Does It Mean to Be Audacious?

To thine own self be true.
~ William Shakespeare

Have you heard someone exclaim, "Well ... the audacity!" about someone who had the nerve to do something bold and perhaps rude? Audacity in the case of Muse-creativity is not disrespect toward other mortals or toward oneself. Audacity's influence includes respect—yet this does not necessarily mean positive public opinion is needed. In fact, one of the favorite things Audacity encourages mortals to say is "Listen, if everyone likes what I've done, I haven't gone far enough to be true to myself. It is not possible to be liked by everyone if I am deeply authentic." And this is perfectly okay.

Oprah Winfrey, a former people-pleaser addict, says that now, if she is being true to herself, there is usually someone mad at her. It is most important for her to follow her intuition as to what is right for her, not the words of others. She seems to have gained massive popularity being true to herself despite those mad at her. She's made a difference.

We love to watch movie characters who demonstrate audacity because then we can vicariously experience their freedom, confidence, and ability to share with the world their earnest convictions in a bold and sometimes outrageous manner. From *Harold and Maude*, Jason Bourne, *Erin Brockovich*, Nancy Drew, *Billy Elliot*, Juliette Binoche's character in *Chocolat* . . . to more recently, *The Marvelous Mrs. Maisel*, June Osborn from *The Handmaids Tale*, Viola Davis in *The Woman King*. They are heroes that go against previous limits of acceptability to stay true to themselves or to their cause.

There are also individuals from whom we can draw audacious energy: Georgia O'Keefe, Frida Kahlo, Harriet Tubman, Malala Yousafzai. I find Chelsea Handler irreverently inspiring most of the time.

Living on the Edge of Freedom

The joy of living comes from not being afraid to risk living fully. This does not mean risking life and limb by taking foolish chances, but rather risking acceptance in order to be real. It means risking being vulnerable and sometimes uncomfortable, in order to be free to act spontaneously. We can never be truly free unless we are fully ourselves.

Gertrude Stein said, "Let me listen to me and not to them." To be true to oneself means ignoring the advice of people who uphold a certain way to do, and to be, as the only way. These are the people who fear change or feel threatened by the creativity of others. Many people care too much about what people think at the expense of sharing their uncommon gifts, unique views, and distinctive lifestyles. They also sacrifice a lifetime of living their sublime destiny.

The Blunderous Phenomenon of Hesitation

Only those who risk going too far know how far they can go. ~ T. S. Eliot

We might also feel we are disdainfully presumptuous if we take creative work we have completed and submit it for publication, show, or sharing. We think that it might not be good enough, or we might be judged and rejected. Yet, many times the only thing that differentiates a successful artist, writer, rugged individualist, is audacity, taking the extra step of sharing and submitting work without the restraint that comes from worrying what people will think.

The cheeky prevail and reap the benefits of courage, notoriety, and growth. These first steps of putting our work and talents out there propel us to better ourselves to meet that mark and then rise to the next. The countless artists and creative individuals who have a standard that must be reached before they are willing to share their work miss out on the experience and amazing insights for growth that come from sharing their work. And the standards they are waiting to achieve may never arrive without the necessary tension of showing their creative expression.

Audacity terms this the "blunderous phenomenon of hesitation." It is a Muse crime requiring the attention of the Creativity Police Force—a faction you do not want to contend with.

We must be willing to fall flat on our face. Fearlessly putting ourselves out there is simply a required part of the creative process. At the very least, it results in the gift of humility and, at best, it's a hell of a lot of fun. Both are pretty good rewards.

You need a little more audacity. When this is the case, pull out this emergency passage from Marianne Williamson's book *A Return to Love*:

> We ask ourselves, who am I to be brilliant, gorgeous, talented and fabulous?
> Actually, who are you not to be? You are a child of God.
> Your playing small doesn't serve the world.
> There is nothing enlightened about shrinking so that other people will not feel insecure around you.
> We were born to make manifest the glory of God that is within us.
> It is not in just some of us; it is in everyone.
> And as we let our own light shine, we unconsciously give people permission to do the same.
> As we are liberated from our own fear, our presence automatically liberates others.

When we are true to our own creative light, others will be true to theirs. If not, they will be left in their shy and shallow places of muck until they are ready to emerge. The Bodyguard tells us we need to be shielded from people who discourage our decision to live a creative life, and the strength to do this needs to come from deep inside. It's there ... use it.

Modesty has its place in the social graces, no doubt. Being humble allows for approachability and refinement. Yet, in moving toward self-realization, it can limit us if it is overused or used inauthentically.

Cultivating Audacity

We all have equal access to the energy of Audacity. This energy animates us to be more "uniquely" ourselves! It starts with a little courage to go beyond what any voices in our head tell us not to do because of fear. After a while, those voices give up when they see we have the courage to act in spite of their taunting. We are free to dance to our own unique music and inspire those who are ready to dance to theirs.

FEARS ARE BALLOONS

Robert Genn, the late painter and on-line columnist, noted that the loss of our power in the creative process can many times be attributed to our fears, fears that "float up in the mind and obstruct the free flow". He suggests that people identify their fears, list them out, and then float them in the air like balloons and pop them. Audacity concurs with this idea and even encourages you to buy or designate your own personal-power sharp thing, decorate it or have a place of honor for it, and pull it out anytime a fear floats up in front of your magnificence.

Robert Genn noted, "The following are multiple choice. There are more. Go for it. Fear of failure. Fear of success. Fear of competition. Fear of play. Fear of joy. Fear of work. Fear of plagiarism. Fear of learning something. Fear of being an impostor. Fear of not being paid. Fear of being paid. Fear of being ridiculed. Fear of being noticed. Fear of not being noticed. Fear of being copied. Fear of making a mess. Fear of being wrong. Fear of the unknown. Fear of commitment. Fear of getting excited. Fear of wasting time. Fear of irrelevance. Fear of fear itself. Pop, pop, pop."

AUDACITY IS COMPASSIONATE TOWARD COMPARISON

Comparing your work, intentions, talents, to others is a sure way to invite a creative clog. It's what we do though as humans. Comparison is one of those temptations on the journey that mortals need to acknowledge as normal but refuse to embrace for more than the minute it takes to realize we're in it.

When you catch yourself in a comparison situation, just think to yourself, "Oh, I'm being human again" and then consider replacing your thought with an affirmation that works for you, such as "I am on my own path and what she/he has done is only proof that I can do it, too", or "I have everything I need and I trust I am moving forward" or, just plain, "So what, that's them, this is me". Ask yourself the question: "What would it feel like to feel as if I am doing just fine just the way I am". Just this question can tame the comparison animal. There will always people whose skills are both greater and lesser than ours… try focusing on the lesser skilled people for a change.

Intuition

Intuition originates from our deepest truth. The discovery of our intuition as the voice of authenticity paves a path clear for us to trust we can express who we are. The discovery of this unique voice of the spirit inside us is, in itself, motivation to share. Sharing ourselves creatively is what we were designed to do. Why else would we all be so different?

Practice your confidence of intuitive knowing:

For a decision you need to make, fill in the following sentences:
- I think ...
- I sense ...
- I know for sure ...

Then write about how it felt to make the distinction between thinking, sensing, and knowing.

Mortals Who Were Inspired by Audacity

As you walk through Audacity's part of the garden, you see her teachings seem to have freed many bridled souls to speak their truth. Notice how you feel more willing to take risks in line with your divine authenticity (and then take one if big and two if small).

> If you pay nervous attention to other people's opinions, maneuver to obtain their indulgence and to stand high in their esteem, you will be whisked about in their winds and you will lose yourself.
> ~ Jo Coubert

> The most common form of despair is not being who you are.
> ~ Søren Kierkegaard

> When you can do the common things of life in an uncommon way, you will command the attention of the world.
> ~ George Washington Carver

MUSE PROFILE OF AUDACITY

SYMBOL

Audacity's symbol is a dazzling marquee sending a message to the world to shamelessly share talents in an authentically personal way.

HOBBIES

Freedom, parades, body painting, tight-rope walking, dancing on tables, baton twirling, performance art, taking fashion risks, inspiring mortals to be themselves with verve, exhibitionism, and talking over a PA system.

> To change one's life:
> Start immediately.
> Do it flamboyantly.
> No exceptions.
> ~ William James, psychologist

AFFIRMATIONS AND SMALL QUESTIONS FROM AUDACITY

- What would it feel like to be true to myself?
- What's one tiny courageous step I can take today?
- As my intuition strengthens, I am confident about the decisions I make.
- I have the courage to express my talents even if it's just 5% more than yesterday.
- I release the restraint of believing taking creative time is selfish. Creative time is divinely spent and makes me a better person for all other areas of my life.
- Being my authentic self is a hell of a lot more fun than trying to be someone else..

And so it is. Audacity is with you.

Journal Check-in

1. Take out your journal and write about where you are with audacity, courage, and authenticity. List examples of audacity in your life.

2. Quickly fill in this blank at least 5 different ways: If I were true to myself I would…
Keep going with this unfinished sentence: With more courage I get to. . .

3. Take a look at the quotes from mortals who were inspired by Audacity in the chapter. Choose one or more and pick up where the quote stops and continue with your own thoughts or simply speed-write about how the quote applies to you.

4. Get comfortable, and close your eyes. Embody the essence of what you know about the Muse Audacity. Feel her strength fill your body. Contact your own Audacity energy and then write a letter to yourself. What would she say specifically to you about being yourself and authenticity? About courage? Let her counter what your critic said. Let her praise your efforts.

Courage is being afraid but going on anyhow. ~Dan Rather

Muse Walk—Audacity Style

Go outside for a meditative walk. Walk with a feeling of courage in your body. Feel a sense of audacity arising from inside you. Think of what you might do if you had ten times more courage than you have now. Do you walk differently when filled with outrageous energy? Do you think differently? Do the neighbors feel greater respect for you?

Brainstorm

Beliefs

Identifying our beliefs strengthens our motivation to boldly be ourselves. Quick List fifteen of your beliefs. They can be as small as "I believe in the blessing of the first sunlight in the morning" to "I believe in world peace." Write them quickly, feeling your conviction for them grow by increasing the pressure of your pen, pencil, or crayon.

"Act As If"

Audacity loves this "act as if" exercise. Act as if you are an artist, a writer, or an authentically expressive person, and you will convince yourself that you truly are and begin to fill the form. During the writing of this book, I consulted a coach to help me focus. She asked me, "What is it that authors do? Find out and do it." It seemed like such an easy concept, but the truth was, I was doing what people who procrastinate do, not what authors do. As soon as I gave myself the label "author" and "acted as if" I were one, confidence surfaced, and the conditions came together to help me to focus on the right activities.

What are five things you can begin "acting as if" in order to weave closer to your dream?

1.
2.
3.
4.
5.

Tips from Audacity

- Explore dropping 5% of your preoccupation with what people think. How's that feel?
- Talk back to your inner critic: Say, "Thanks for sharing now, bye-bye!" Replace their voice with the word: Onward!
- Share your art, submit your writing, share dance, music, song, and reap the benefits of strengthening your character. Share at an open-mike event.
- Do those things that your heart desires without guilt, apology, or self-consciousness.

- Give yourself permission to do these things imperfectly and in a small, non-linear way.. 5% more each time.

In your journal, claim what you do really well—bypassing your inner critic and releasing inferiority, insecurity, false modesty. Write boldly. Use a permanent marker.

List five of your audacious-fantasy personalities. Give them a name, a hobby, or an occupation. Here are some of mine:

Disagreement Diva: Is not afraid to disagree with someone at the risk of making him or her mad.
Ballsie Betty: Pulls a chair up to a table of strangers in a restaurant and is so charming they buy her dinner.
Monica: Jumps out of birthday cakes and throws frosting at the onlookers.
Angie: Is a fireman.
Rocky Renee: Ushers mothers who mistreat their kids to the bathroom for a good talking to.
Angela: Paints with pistachio, banana, and cherry pudding on white linen pants and wears them to the grocery store.

Make a list of ten or more preferences that, at least for today, you want to claim for your own (e.g., I like vanilla shakes better than chocolate, I prefer tulips to carnations, I like reading better than football, I like plays better than opera, I like *The Grinch Who Stole Christmas* better than *A Charlie Brown Christmas*). This helps you make a small stand for the moment, empowering the convictions of your authentic identity.

Give yourself the title that feels like the courageous you—artist, writer, screenwriter, woman extraordinary, Warrior Princess, Brilliant Decorator, Titillating Conversationalist, Chocolate Cake Olympic Gold Medalist, Sensual Goddess, Love God.

SIGN HERE WITH YOUR NAME AND YOUR TITLE:

☆ _____ ☆

Next Stop in the Garden

As you walk farther down the path, you come to a hammock. Here, stretched out in the bliss of reverie, is yet another Muse. The trees have lost their leaves and the weather creates dormancy. It is the winter of creativity—the creative cycle decrees rest, diversional activities are encouraged, and catching the breath is in order. During the pause, the grace of gratitude is also addressed.

Come and sit in the lull between the labor. Submit to the influence of letting go. Upon return, you will then be refilled with the fuel of dreams, with a renewed perspective, and often a clear sense of what needs to come next. Ideas will be more immediate if not virtually parading around you for your attention. "Yo! Over here!" New energy and fresh approaches will make your ideas sparkle. Accept rest.

LULL:
MUSE OF PAUSE, DIVERSION, AND GRATITUDE

To do great work a man must be very idle as well as very industrious.
~ Samuel Butler, English novelist, satirist

Summon Lull When:

- You are having a creative dry spell.

- You are stuck in similar themes, repeating previous ideas, and having difficulty coming up with something new.

- You feel creatively blocked, burnt out or you've come face-to-face with a quagmire.

- You are losing energy toward, or have stopped enjoying, your creative passion.

Bottom Line

Sometimes in the creative process, the next right step is to let go, pause, and give time for our vast resources to connect and spring into new ideas. Surrender to the natural cycle of creativity. Fill with new sensations. Meditate. Turn your attention to mind-stimulating activities. Let go of trying to control things. Trust in the process. Celebrate the creative rejuvenation of rest and pause. Say thanks.

The Selection of Lull

The Muses were working incredibly hard to reinvent themselves into these modern versions of the Greek inspiration brokers. They had successfully come up with five Muses when, *zap*! Muse revamping came to an abrupt halt. They still had some slots left to fill, but they could not think of what would work next. They made all sorts of facial contortions, had a few brain strains, and Bea Silly's attention span was completely shot. They tried hard to control the process by auditioning various Muses, hiring a Muse from an escort service, and attempting to rehabilitate a Muse with a bad reputation. They were trying too hard—then it dawned on them: "Duh! We need a break!"

As often as it happened, they were still surprised when the juices dried up without warning. So they took a break. One of them went skiing in the French Alps for a while, and one of them lay in the grass and looked at the pale moon in the daytime sky, but most were fine with just being still. They just stopped doing what they were doing to rest, to let go, to listen, and to receive. That's how they came up with the next new Muse, Lull.

Your Lull Energy

The word lull, according to the mortal Word-Weaver, Webster, means "quiet, stillness, pause, short period of calm; to bring repose, rest." The Muse Lull embodies and inspires all these definitions in the interest of the release that mortals need when their brains get stuck. It is a time of no action, of listening, of releasing, and when the time is right, of receiving.

In addition, a creative lull is a time to look in a different direction to activities unrelated to the primary creative passion, process, or problem. It is the phase of a cycle that involves turning away and filling the inner well with more experiences, sensations, and emotions from which to draw upon, enticing back creative vitality, direction, and insight.

The lack of directed thought that comes during a creative break creates a chance for ideas to connect on a subconscious level. Breaks result in "eureka" experiences of solutions, plans, or definitive directions. Profound discoveries make regular appearances during a pause. This is the mystery of inspiration, and one of the joys of being a creative mortal.

Lull lets us know that at certain points in our creative process we cannot make more progress unless we honor the part of the cycle where the unconscious processes of spirit and intellect have a chance to connect. Sometimes when we go blank, it is simply Lull reaching to replenish the resources of our creative magic.

> I handle the notes no better than many others,
> but the pauses—ah! that is where the art resides.
> ~ Arthur Rubinstein

Taking A Break

Kerry Vesper, a wood sculptor and furniture maker in Tempe, Arizona, says he struggles with a problem until he starts repeating himself. "At that point I let it go," he says. "I put it away and do something else."

Feed the Brain

The mind's bank of resources is another magical and enigmatic quality of the creative process. Our subconscious collection of universal themes is also tapped. The richer the depth of our experience, whether it be in the inner world or the external world, the more we have to pull from in order to invent, create, and self-express.

We can overdraw from that bank of resources. This will cause creative dry spells, stale ideas, and blocks. So during our breaks, we need to refill. This is one of the principles of Julia Cameron's powerful experience of creative recovery in *The Artist's Way*. She prescribes a weekly "Artist's Date", an hour's worth of solitary and festive excursion. During such events the Artist Way followers experience synchronicity, the seeming coincidence of events whose relevance to our needs is uncanny.

When we feel overdrawn, the Muses recommend "diversional" activities to restore creative abundance. This comes in the form of any experience that diverts our attention from our intense work and that is desired by the artist child inside us. Lull calls it the Surreptitious Adventures of Sacred Solitude (SASS). She calls it SASS to conjure up the attitude of secret self-adventure, which makes the experience entice us with fun and appealing adventure. But you can call it whatever you wish… just give yourself this time and watch the magic.

Gratitude

Gratitude has a compelling role in creativity. Energetically, we repel matter when we are needy. We repel situations, people, and interestingly enough, creative inspiration. When we shift our thinking and have a sense of appreciation, we fill, and from a filled place we have a desire to share our joy and creative expression. Studies have proven, over and over, that mortals in a positive state of mind create more than those who are negative. You can be sad, angry, and regretful, but when you know that creativity is an outlet that helps… that's where your positive thought brings you to expression.

Meditation

Meditation is not as elusive and out of reach as many people seem to think. I use meditation more than any other method to access ideas for writing, paintings, performance art, classes, and issues needing creative problem solving. Meditation is a time to focus on the present moment and clear the mind so that our divine creative resources from within can find and fill the void. It can also be a time to say thanks.

Once you start meditating regularly, you will discover the incredible effect it has on centering you and opening your mind—but do not expect it to be easy at the beginning. Quieting the mind is a skill, and just like art, music, or acting, it requires patience and practice. Have no expectations, no judgments about your practice. Accept where you are, will often be like listening to the running commentary of your mind. When it has not been trained to release the control it has over you, the mind will intrude soon after you have just quieted it. This is normal and is not a product of your particular oddness or inability. Feel triumphant when you catch it, warmly welcome yourself back, and begin again. This is practice for "beginning again" after the many ways the dark factions of creativity can derail or discourage us.

In the mystic calm of your inner world, you will more easily open to the voice of intuition and draw upon the vast resources of your inner wisdom.

> Sometimes I sits and thinks. And sometimes I just sits.
> ~Satchel Paige

Empty White Space To Rest In

Mortals Who Were Inspired by Lull

Wow, a lot of mortals have been influenced by these Muses already. You can truly savor what Lull has inspired mortals to say:

> If you're having difficulty coming up with new ideas, then slow down.
> ~ Natalie Goldberg

> In the depth of winter, I finally learned that within me there lay an invincible summer.
> ~ Albert Camus

> It takes a lot of time to be a genius; you have to sit around so much doing nothing, really doing nothing.
> ~ Gertrude Stein

> Yet it is in our idleness, in our dreams, that the submerged truth comes to the top.
> ~ Virginia Woolf

Muse Profile of Lull

Symbol

Lull's symbol is a hammock filled with flowers, symbolic of a place to rest, daydream, and ponder the fullness of our existence.

Hobbies

Lull's hobbies are pausing, daydreaming, meditating, loitering, seeking out atypical festive experiences, climbing trees, watching a play, reading obscure magazines, visiting a nursery, lying on the grass looking at the clouds through the trees.

Affirmations and Small Questions from Lull

🌀 What does rest or a creative break look like and feel like to me?

- What idea is calling for me to daydream about it and where might a daydream lead it?

- I release the creative process and trust that inspirations are on their way to me now.

- I trust that letting go will bring me back to my creative productivity even if just 5% more.

- I enjoy this space between creative activities and fill myself with new experiences, sensations, and feelings that result in a fresh creative flow.

- I am thankful for the abundance already in my life.

- I get to take a few minutes today to tune in to my inner self.

And there ya go. And your Lull energy is awakened.

JOURNAL CHECK-IN

1. Take out your journal and write, draw, or paint about where you are with Lull: How is your Lull energy? Have you allowed yourself to feel the sensations of a colorful diversion? Are you able to let go and let it be?

2. Continue one or all of these unfinished sentences: In the space between the worlds… When I let go… Give your inner critic the day off.

3. Write as if you were a "lull," talk about your qualities and intentions, e.g., I am a lull, a pause pregnant with possibility. I float through space and land on flowers . . . I dream of meadows with dancing light . . . Something like that.

4. Look at the quotes by mortals who were inspired by Lull throughout the chapter and pick one. Continue the essence of the quote in your own words or simply speed-write how the quote applies to you.

5. Write as if you were Lull talking to you. What would she say specifically to you about taking breaks, meditating, giving thanks, and finding ways to

refresh yourself with new experiences? What do you need to learn from her purpose and powers? Have her compliment you on how you are including her in your life and counter what the critic said above.

Muse Walk—Lull Style

Stop and go for a walk. Choose someplace different to walk. Find a different part of your neighborhood, or walk your usual walk backward. Wear something different when you walk. Walk through a store you don't usually walk through. Walk through a clothes store and buy something different. Embody the sense of someone who has truly let go of whatever process is the focus of your life right now. Or do not walk this time, just sit instead.

Brainstorm

Regular Walking

If you are seeking creative ideas, go out walking. Angels whisper to a man when he goes for a walk. ~ Raymond Imon

Natalie Goldberg walks her dogs for inspiration. Wolfgang Amadeus Mozart said he could hear his compositions all at once, "in a pleasing, lively dream" while he walked. Poet A. E. Housman said this about a brisk walk: "As I went along, thinking nothing in particular . . . there would flow into my mind with sudden and unaccountable emotion, sometimes a line or two of verse, sometimes a whole stanza at once." All sorts of revelations happen during walking. Take a notepad, pen, or recording device with you!

Meditation

Practice consciously associating empowering messages with your breathing for a while, and soon your breath will be the automatic circulation of effortless, ongoing positive fuel.

Examples:

- Inhale and allow yourself to fully receive this inhale as if it were a beautiful inspiration. Fully feel every sensation of the inhale.

- Exhale with a feeling of letting go, releasing control, surrendering the need to be constantly doing something.

SURREPTITIOUS ADVENTURES OF SACRED SOLITUDE (SASS)

- Steal away into your bathroom with fragrant bath oils, salts, and bubbles. Light candles, play music. Take your time. Do this twice a day if necessary. Let your mind be as light as the bubbles. Feel the warmth of the water and the body's inner recognition of being nurtured.

- Take a walk on the beach, in a garden, through a garden nursery. Give yourself $25 to spend however you wish. Practicality is not a requirement.

- Go to the theater or some other event by yourself and notice the explosion of new sensations you feel when you are not in the more contained world of being with another person.

- Load the cooler with cold drinks and sandwiches, get in the car, put on some favorite playlists, and just drive, destination unknown.

- Or, drive to a nearby town and explore.

- Put some music on or listen to audiobooks or podcasts while making a collage, watercolor, or finger painting.

☆ Take a walk accompanied with small, curious questions, like "What message is out here for me today?", "What creative call is about to look me up?" (let go of the need to have an answer).

☆ Take the day off and switching up your routine.

☆ Walk in a bookstore, asking a question and opening a book randomly to find the answer.

☆ Go to an art gallery. Go to the art gallery gift shop.

Next Stop in the Garden

You are noticing that the creative journey is bringing up some uncomfortable feelings. You feel like eating more, watching more TV, or biting your nails. You are discovering parts of yourself that you do not really want to know, or new parts that are unrecognizable from the former definition you had of yourself. Your avoidance strategies are spinning—but you hold on in order to check out the mystery. Since you met Albert, you realize that there is a new way to look at things. And as you walk on the garden path and think this, your shadow grows long and you turn to see that your shadow is actually a Modern Day Muse, too.

Raw creative energy has been known to come from a mortal's darkness, so the Muses added a Shadow to remind you to alchemize the darkness into art and personal freedom. Underneath our veneer of "nice" is another side that is ready to release some really juicy creativity. The Shadow Muse dares you to come closer and examine a side of yourself that you may not realize is alive with possibilities.

SHADOW:
MUSE OF THE DARK SIDE

SUMMON THE SHADOW MUSE WHEN

- You want to explore the potential of creativity contained within "the dark side" of your personality.

- You are prone to dark moods, pain, and sensitivities that you would like to metabolize into poignant self-expression or to see in creative perspective as gifts of strength.

- You are curious about the fine line between creativity and madness.

- You want to activate compassion for the common humanity that is present when we are in the undesirable parts of ourselves.

BOTTOM LINE

Shedding light on our darkest qualities releases the energy of creativity. Honoring all the aspects of that which we are, rewards us with compassion, and insight. Revel in your rarities. Release the restraint of your insecure ego. Find art and freedom in your Shadow.

THE SHADOW SELECTION

The Modern Day Muses were almost finished coming up with the upgraded versions of the original nine Muses. They were on number eight. They wanted the next Muse to have a little depth—some intrigue—be a bit mysterious. And they thought and they thought.

And then the Muses started to get a little crazy and sinister. The side of each of them that is naughty and not-so-much-nice started to appear. They rather became controlling, intolerant, and one of them started spitting. Personality blemishes broke out in complaining, whining, and not making sense. And in the midst of the darkness, they noticed the creative brilliance that's possible when our slips are showing. Hence, the Shadow Muse came into being.

Your Shadow Energy

The dark sides of personalities are always present, just as light invariably casts a shadow. When the light is brightest, the shadow is deepest. When mortals explore their hidden shadow side, there is a power, a liberating freedom, and a creative release. Carl Jung opened mortals to this idea, and the Muses want to elaborate in the interest of creative expression.

The Potential of Creativity Contained in Your Shadow

Keeping the aspects of ourselves that we do not like suppressed encloses us in a restricted space of awareness. Keeping the less desirable sides of ourselves out of sight takes a lot of energy. Exploring this shadow side to the point of acknowledging and accepting our disowned parts can give us a tremendous release of energy, freedom, and power. Acknowledging, accepting, and integrating that energy can result in a new lease on life and can open a reservoir of creative expression—not to mention acceptance, compassion, and forgiveness.

Viewing our weaknesses with compassion and possibility is profoundly liberating. It gives us another creative mechanism with which to deal with life's complexities and the pursuit of living deeply. We can embrace the world with a lightness of being and witness the beauty of our humanity.

Metabolizing Pain into Poignant Self-Expression

Many people find that creative release comes easier in times of poignant emotion: after a romantic breakup, a loss, during moments of anger or confusion. All of a sudden, words and images flow, or expressing one's pain is simply easier. Sorrow and anger lay dormant much of the time, so when unexpected hard times break through the defenses, the emotions sometimes spill forth in beautiful words, visions, music, feeling, and insights. Paul Simon said, "My words trickle down from a wound I have no intention to heal." Alan DeNiro said, "Fall in love, then have a breakup. Plenty of writing material there." What wounds do you have that can serve your soul through creative expression?

Madness and Creativity

Creativity that tarries on the edge of sanity is the breath of daring. It is the uninhibited display of the unseen, unsaid, and the not yet experienced. Loose ego boundaries can set free the avant-garde.

Hieronymus Bosch, surrealism, dadaism, Edvard Munch, and other unconventional art and artists have a sense of madness to them. Expressionists and abstract artists such as Pollock and countless others broke tradition by sublimating their madness in revolutionary new forms born of their deep inner turmoil. Musicians from Tchaikovsky to The Doors have elevated derangement to art. Listening gifts us with poignant effects unrealizable through sanity. Creativity is both a strategy and sublimation for inner turmoil.

> It is under these immense stretches of wheat, under these troubled skies, that I am unhindered in expressing deep sorrow and extreme solitude. ~ Vincent Van Gogh

Mortals Who Were Inspired by the Shadow Muse

This part of the garden is dark. Wandering branches of towering oak trees that reach in all directions have Spanish moss blowing from their limbs in forewarning. It's at once ominous and beautiful. Mortals touched by the Shadow Muse lend their voices to these ponderings.

> It is, after all, the dab of grit that seeps into an oyster's shell that makes the pearl, not pearl-making seminars with other oysters.
> ~ Stephen King

> Conflict ... that's where we find art.
> ~ Garrison Keillor

> "Creativity - like human life itself - begins in darkness." ~ Julia Cameron

> "Comedy equals tragedy plus time."
> ~Mark Twain

MUSE PROFILE OF THE SHADOW MUSE

SYMBOL

The Shadow's symbol is a window looking upon the moonlight amidst a dark night. As Allen Ginsberg says, "Follow your inner moonlight: don't hide the madness."

HOBBIES

Opening closet doors, playing evocative music, materializing mirrors for a closer look, inviting mortals to walk through the darkness and to find the light.

> Everyone has talent. What is rare is the courage to follow the talent to the dark place where it leads.
> ~ Erica Jong, author

AFFIRMATIONS FROM THE SHADOW MUSE

☾ I allow the voice of creativity to express through my emotions.

☾ I'd like things in my world to be different, but they're not, and that's okay.

☾ As I discover and accept my dark side, I build compassion and feel a sense of union with all mankind. We all have darkness, and we all have light. I bigger than my past mistakes.

☾ I have the courage to explore my pain and my fears.

And so it is. And the Shadow Muse is here to free you.

Revealing the dark side of human nature has been, then, one of the primary purposes of art and literature.

JOURNAL CHECK-IN

Marybeth Webster, a Grass Valley, California, art therapist, who often works with artists, says writing in a journal can often clear a creative block. "In a journal, you set aside time to focus on yourself, and there's a freedom to tell the truth," she says. "It's a real opportunity to face the shadow." To break through an agonizing writing block, she kept a journal to record her dreams.

1. Take out your journal and write about where you are with the Shadow Muse in your life. What is your dark side like?

2. Look over the quotes by mortals who were inspired by the Shadow Muse, (throughout the chapter). Pick one that has a special charge for you and continue where it stops or write how it applies to you.

3. Write, paint, or draw as if you were the dark side of the world.

4. Take a moment to relax and embody the essence of your own Shadow Muse from what you have learned about it. Then write yourself a letter as if the Shadow Muse were speaking. How would she encourage you in drawing on your dark side? What would she praise you for in your shadow work?

Muse Walk—Shadow Style

Stop right here. Go outside for a meditative walk. Embody the Shadow side of yourself in your walk and your posture. Let yourself view the world from your dark side. What do you feel? Write about it when you get back or dictate into your smart phone.

Dipping into Your Shadow

Reverse Psychology

If you give yourself just five minutes a day to feel fully guilty, shame, or that which you criticize yourself continuously— without trying to placate yourself with pleasantries—many times this release of resistance creates a thoroughfare for the thoughts to get through, completely disarms the feeling, and lets it pass through without its toxic toll.

Whatever it is that torments you about yourself, know you're not alone. It's common humanity to be hard on ourselves. Consider practicing compassion for being the kind of person 1) who is hard on themselves, and 2) whatever it is you feel is undesirable. Compassion, according to scientist, Kristin Neff, cultivates strength, coping skills, resilience, AND creativity, more than harsh self-criticism.

> *"I think songwriting is the ultimate form of being able to make anything that happens in your life productive." ~ Taylor Swift*

Next Stop in the Garden

So you are walking along your garden path thinking, "It's not like I don't want to engage in creative ideas, I have wanted to do it all along. Creativity is definitely a priority; the only problem is I don't seem to be doing it. I am having problems getting started."

You are not alone. Creative-ignition difficulties are more common than stuffed-up noses. The Muses are here to help clear your passages.

One of the Greek Muses updated herself into a reliable, strong, and focused straight shooter, boycotting the whims of moods, the paralysis of perfection, or the distraction of anything that steals mortals from their creative passion. She has been here all along in the discussion of small steps, but now we get to meet her and benefit from her wisdom and influence.

> Bob Moawad says, "You can't make footprints in the sands of time if you're sitting on your butt, and who wants to make buttprints in the sands of time?"

MARGE:
MUSE OF OKAY-NOW-LET'S-GET-STARTED

It's a job that's never started that takes the longest to finish.
~ J.R.R. Tolkien, author

SUMMON MARGE WHEN

❧ You are having a hard time getting started on your creative passion. Resistance and procrastination seduce you to their place of discontent. Your avoidance strategies are impressively well cultivated.

- You are overwhelmed with the task before you—you feel immobilized, frozen, inert, and not quite sure where to start, so you reconsider starting at all.
- Chances are good that you will just give up or put your creative passion off indefinitely even if the voice of inspired reason continues to call to you.
- You always read books on creativity, but do none of what they recommend.

Bottom Line

We all have a way to be creative that can make the world a better place even if it's just putting ourselves in a better mood. There are many things that can steal us from creative expression, and we have the choice to do our work anyway. The discipline to engage in our passions can be made easy with routine, reasonable goals, small steps, and focus. The result is that what we are meant to create comes to life.

The Selection of Marge

In 1996, the Muses went to see the movie *Fargo*. In the movie, an unflappable sheriff named Marge Gunderson resolves the gnarly crimes that happen in North Dakota, despite her challenges of pregnancy, snow, dense deputies, and an uncooperative car salesman. Marge's no-nonsense Midwestern attitude gets the job started and, without moodiness, complaints, or drama, gets the job done. The Muses feel they ended up going to that movie because the Marge character was a good inspiration for a Muse. Stoicism can actually move us past the drama that holds our energy hostage.

Your Marge Energy: Must-see Creativity

Planning on starting a creative project and instead finding yourself removing fleas from your dog? Are you on-line shopping, playing on-line games, and scrolling on social media when you intended to write? Putting projects off until you have "a block of time" that never seems to arrive because there's a new mini-series on Netflix?

You have fallen prey to the avoidance dilemma. When you are in avoidance, you wear earplugs and can't hear what your good intentions are trying to tell you. You get a lot of cleaning done.

Sometimes we avoid creativity because we do not want to do something that is not as easy to manage as the remote control. Other reasons are not as simple to figure out, mainly because we are not even conscious of them. How can we be so resistant to a process that we were so excited about at the beginning? Or why don't we finish the projects we were so agog about when we started? An invisible force grips our good intentions and threatens them until they give in to "must-see TV". Yet, the voice inside lobbying for creative expression persists, and you still squirm with a guilt you cannot hide. When you ignore the ideas that chose you for their vehicle of expression, chances are that you will wear unrest like a perpetual itch.

> It does not matter how slowly you go, so long as you do not stop.
> ~ Confucius, Chinese philosopher

Many mortals struggle with getting started on their creative passions because of pressure. Creativity goes deep into the well of who we are, dipping us into the unknown, which is sometimes scary—and "sometimes scary" is a stimulus for resistance. Are you resistant?

Creativity taps into our deepest insecurities. This is good. Fear is a sure indicator that we are in store for growth if we accept the call to go beyond the mundane and into new possibilities strewn in the unrevealed. When we surrender the safety and security of the known for the precarious unpredictability of the unknown, our strength, confidence, compassion, and self-knowledge cannot help but grow. The creative journey brings up fear. Fear of exposure, fear of failure, fear of inadequacy, fear of undeserved good things, fear of responsibility, and fear of hard work. All of these fears may rear their prickly heads at the onset of creative acts. Creativity requires a change in patterns that don't serve us. Even a positive change from negative patterns can result in resistance when we are unsure of the new ground on which we stick our big exploratory toe.

The Muses have spent endless nights devising solutions, potions, and resistance removers in Muse laboratories because the problem seems widespread. Frankly, it really infuriates the Muses. They hate to be ignored when they send out sizzling sparks of epiphanies. An infuriated Muse is not a pretty sight.

Marge Sez, "Well, Okeydoke Then"

Marge's approach is definitive but nonjudgmental. Connecting with action is the only thing that will guarantee to get mortals going creatively. Marge responds to moods, insecurities, distractions, habits, addictions, over-responsibility, or the illusion of not having enough time preventing you from getting going by saying, "Gee, thanks a bunch for sharing, but I've got a date with my creativity. So, I appreciate the offer, but I'm gonna have to turn you down." Do the same and then set yourself in action. Do not look back. Do not dust the top of your refrigerator.

Habits

If you engage in your creative passion five minutes "dailyish" for three weeks, you will have created a daily routine. Habits are helpful in keeping the creative progression going.

If you are not taking regular classes in your creative passion, creating a habit is the next easiest way to maintain creativity in your daily schedule and keep it there. And if you are not in the habit of getting right into your work, do not expect that it will be easy. "Starting" gets easier the more you do it. But at the beginning it is like a huge aircraft taking off. It requires a lot of momentum ... it rolls slowly down the runway until it lifts off the ground and is on its way.

Creativity is responsible for our mental, emotional, and spiritual vitality. Thus, a daily habit of creativity is vital to our fulfilled existence. A routine similar to teeth brushing deserves installation into the daily schedule. Consider creativity hygiene for your soul.

Mornings work for many artists ... getting up a little earlier is a sacred act that becomes easier as the momentum of the ritual takes over. Performing your creative passion first thing in the morning is a message that the sacred act of creativity comes first. However, several artists observed by Marge agreed that any time you can make regular is a good time. At first, be prepared to use a little awkward force to start the routine. That's okay, persistence is the key to success. Your work will have a time and space to flourish slowly and dependably. Over time, you will generate and refine abundant creative output. The heavens will applaud and you will indeed experience the miracles that creativity bestows.

To honor the routine completely, and to diminish the pressure, sometimes the starting place is simply showing up. If you decide your routine is to work from 7:45 to 8:00 A.M., the requirement is to be there, even if you are just sitting and staring. Do this dailyish without worrying if you skip a day.

> For of all sad words of tongue or pen, the saddest are these:
> "It might have been!"
> ~ John Greenleaf Whittier

Honoring a routine, whether or not you feel like it, is the most consistent key to success.

I produce more consistently when I am taking an inspiring class. When in a class, those around me create an energy that inspires my diligence. I also do better with a deadline. I work amazingly well when I'm working at the same time someone else who agreed to work with me is working too (I call this Parallel Universe Time). Knowing these truths about myself gives me options to use when I am struggling to get started.

IGNITION

Just as appetite comes by eating, so work brings inspiration, if inspiration is not discernible at the beginning. ~ Igor Stravinsky

If you are waiting to get in the mood for creativity before you begin your work or start your changes, you may be waiting a long time. Sometimes after Aha-phrodite's energy opens your eyes to a new inspiration, you will feel driven to begin. Sometimes there is no inspiration . . . until you begin. Many times, in fact, the act of beginning starts the inspiration flowing and you wonder what took you so long in the first place. Action begets action. Motion creates inspiration. Keep the pen, the brush, and the intention in motion, and it will soon reward you with inspiration that keeps you going.

Even if you are on the right track, you'll get run over if you just sit there.
~ Will Rogers

MARGE'S STARTER KIT

Often the best way to produce a block is to sit down with a blank sheet of paper and expect inspiration. When you have empirical proof of which of these tools work best for you, list them artistically or with your favorite font on a four-by-six- or five-by-seven-inch piece of paper, buy a fun little frame, and keep it in your workspace.

☆ Listening to a podcast, reading a book, or watch a YouTube that inspires you to begin on your own.

☆ Write a letter from the project to you, having it tell you the next step.

☆ Scribbling nonsense words to get the pen going. Reading from one of your favorite authors.

- ☆ Talk about it to a trusted friend or creativity coach. Talking out loud creates different pathways in the brain and will elicit insight you do not get from thinking.

- ☆ Listening to lyrics of a song that inspires you.

- ☆ Flipping through art magazines, postcards, catalogs, Pinterest, or unrelated sources to see how they can inspire you (without comparing and for just a few seconds if you're easily overwhelmed).

- ☆ Looking at work you've already done to reignite your passion.

- ☆ Taking a walk with an idea.

- ☆ Taking an outing and letting everything you see give you potential ideas about your project. Taking a drive, a shower, a shave, with your idea.

- ☆ Visualizing, with as much detail as possible, your project finished and the feeling of accomplishment and satisfaction you will feel.

- ☆ Remembering that your project will be a beacon of inspiration for others.

- ☆ Remembering what energizes you about your creative passion and slipping into that energy.

- ☆ Listing the next steps for your project and then embarking upon them, one bite-size step at a time.

- ☆ Focusing on one step a day, making it a hard one; getting it out of the way first thing in the morning often creates a feeling of fulfillment and motivation that carries over to more tasks.

- ☆ Here's something sneaky: If you're procrastinating on one project, begin another one and when you get to the hard part of it, procrastinate by going to the project you're really wanting to work on. Repeat and your procrastination will disintegrate.

INFINITESIMALLY SMALL BABY STEPS

> Small actions are at the heart of kaizen.
> By taking steps so tiny that they seem trivial or even laughable, you'll sail calmly past obstacles that have defeated you before.
> ~ Robert Maurer

Feeling overwhelmed is another creativity stopper. Our society, as a whole, has adopted the let's-make-things-really-high-pressure practice. We want everything now and we set our goals too high too soon to be reasonable. We have good intentions, but why try if it is too hard to complete?

Small goals are easily met. We like to be the taskmasters from hell and set lofty goals, which then backfire on us. They are too lofty to even attempt to try. If we did a little at a time, we would get there. When we give up because our only goal is unrealistic, we do not even get close. When a small goal is met, a feeling of success ensues. Success releases motivation and increases interest. More action is likely to occur when success is reachable. Here's the equation:

small goals met = a feeling of success = beaming motivation = increased interest
in dreams and pursuits = more small goals set = advancement toward dreams =
celebration and gratitude and an occasional "Yes!" = results

This is Marge's "Most Treasured Trick": BREAK IT WAAAAAAY DOWN. That's six A's in WAAAAAAY, emphasizing the importance of really, really, really, really, really, really small steps. Change your definition of small to even smaller. And I say this because this is a central blockbuster with the private clients and classroom students with whom I work. Even when I ask, "So, what is your next really, really small step?" they still respond with something too unrealistic for starting up a creative process. Keep breaking it down smaller until it's hard NOT to do it.

Once, I asked one client to set a writing goal for the following week. She replied, "The completion of a chapter." This may be a good goal for an experienced writer, but an unrealistic goal for the newcomer or the returning writer. She came back with no progress. My counter goal for her was one page of awful writing. She came back with a solid first draft of five pages.

Persevere

Simply stated, perseverance is one of the most important parts of not only being successful creatively but in gaining the confidence and skill, so you enjoy the process no matter where it leads. Stay with it.

"Yeah, I Got Time"

Asking questions: There's always time to ask yourself a question, when you first wake up, on a walk, during the morning commute. Asking questions are one of the most powerful catalysts to not only thinking creatively but cultivating the desire to want to get to work.

Short amounts of time: Five to fifteen minutes a day can fit into anyone's schedule, and it really is all the time you need to work toward creative excellence.

Just set up your easel. Let the paintbrush lead you to where it wants to go for fifteen minutes. Do this four times a week, and on the second week look for an image that might want to be painted. Experiment for just fifteen minutes.

- ! Take one prop and experiment with it five minutes for a performance art piece.

- ! Work on finishing that quilt for just five minutes.

- ! Begin your interior decorating passion by looking at a magazine or on the internet for, yes, five minutes.

- ! Next goal would be to wander in a store and get ideas and write them down.

These small goals actually get people excited about starting. Rather than dreading what and how much to do, and wondering if what they have done is enough, small goals motivate people. Then, they are more likely to continue and gradually build the momentum they need to finish. Excitement is what the Muses want you to have. That is what makes the process so precious.

> Sometimes intending to take a 30 second step is enough to break through the resistance to getting started.
>
> It is a matter of persistence and faith and hard work. So you might as well just go ahead and get started.
> ~ Anne Lamott

Muse Profile of Marge

Symbol

Marge's symbol is the release of an arrow toward a bull's-eye (action to goal).

Hobbies

Accomplishment. Being, doing, having. Eating.

Affirmations and Small Questions from Marge

❀ What's one small step I can take today in just 5 minutes?

❀ What's one small thought I can be having about my creative project?

❀ What small reward will motivate me to take a small step, or will taking the step itself be a reward?

❀ What would make it easier to engage in my creative passions?

❀ I am inspired and energized to start working on my creative endeavor.

❀ Okeedokee, I'm getting started now.

Well, alrighty then. Enjoy the process.

JOURNAL CHECK-IN

1. Take out your journal and write about what you know about your own experience of the Muse Marge. What thoughts did reading the chapter bring up for you? Continue with this sentence: To get started…

2. Complete these sentences quickly five times: I'll make it easier to get started by…

3. In just five minutes I can… [on second thought… just go do five minutes of my creative pursuit]

4. Look over the quotes by mortals who were inspired by Marge, throughout the chapter; Pick one that has a special charge for you and continue where it stops or speed-write how it applies to you.

5. Take a moment to relax and embody your own essence of the Muse Marge. From what you have learned about her and know about her powers already present within you, write yourself a letter from her. How would she encourage you in the area of getting started? What would she praise you for? How would she counter the voice of the inner critic?

MUSE WALK—MARGE STYLE

Go outside for a meditative walk. Feel your own getting-started power grow. Think about what project you are working on and what next small step you will take. Picture yourself doing it. Make an analogy of your taking steps in your walk with taking the next steps in your creative passion. Taking one step at a time, feel the quality of moving toward your destination. Feel the confidence of action running through you, and when you return, go straight to the project or process you are working on and do one small part of it—or clean the workspace for it.

> "I long to accomplish a great and noble task, but it is my chief duty to accomplish small tasks as if they were great and noble."
> ~ Helen Keller, author, lecturer

Taking a Class

Many people take classes primarily because the structure of having a place to go for creative expression helps them just do it. People often respond to the structure of time, space, and the energy of other people engaged in working that the classroom situation provides. If classes have worked for you before, make it a routine to check out online and in-person class schedules. Make sure the teacher is one who is validating and inspiring, not dismissive and derailing. Find the class you relate to the most.

Parallel Universe Time

Go beyond being social with your friends and be creative together. Find times that work best for all concerned, then meet weekly, bimonthly, monthly.

The parallel-buddy system: Set up a time that a friend and you can work on your separate projects. The energy of working together gives the work staying power. This works even if your workplaces are in your separate homes in distant spaces. Simply decide on a time to begin and end. Call your friend before you start and at the end of the time limit. Start small. Compare notes about how much was done and how you felt. Chances are you will have created momentum so keep the check-in call at the end short and keep going. Even reward each other. Knowing that someone else is working at the same time will help you work more effectively. Parallel universe time can have a magical feeling to it.

A Creativity Coach

If you want to advance more quickly toward your creative goals, a creativity coach can help. A creativity coach differs from a life coach in that the deadlines a creativity coach sets honor the nonlinear, unpredictable nature of creativity. Kaizen-Muse Creativity Coaches offer experiences during the session itself and hold a supportive space that does not require perfection. Methods also include the activation of intuition, imagination and confidence in guided imageries, tools that make creativity easier to engage in, as well as prescriptions from the Muses geared toward your individual needs.

FIND YOUR PASSION

If you have been courting your true passion, it will not leave you alone until you engage in it. Doing what you love just makes you want to do it more. There is nothing like wanting to spring out of bed in the morning to see the work of art, the writing, the craft—the results of what you started or finished the night before. A little creative foreplay creates the heat that lures more action. If you do not know what your passion is, explore various media. Focus on play.

HAVE A CAUSE

Consider making something creative for the purpose of making someone else feel better. Get involved in a higher cause. It will get you started, and the energy will flow to other areas of your work or it will simply feel good to be devoting your efforts to something generous or that which you believe in.

THE NO-NONSENSE TOOL

The Midwestern value of committing oneself, to get to the work no matter what, will create better efficiency for our creative process. Great self-respect and the reward of moving forward result in the adoption of this value.

Be there in a jiff.
~ The character Marge from the movie Fargo

NEXT STOP IN THE GARDEN

Here at this point in the garden you see a bench. You sit and all of a sudden it dawns on you that you, too, have inspirational abilities. It is a time of self-reflection as you strengthen your knowledge of yourself as the creative being you are. Celebrate yourself as the muse you are.

What Muse Are You?

NAME YOURSELF AND YOUR POWERS

Okay, here are some questions for you. In your journal or sketchbook answer the following: Which of the Muses do you identify with the most? Who else? (If you were representing a Muse, which one would your qualities best be able to match with?)

Which of the Muses would you choose to assist you in deepening your skills or overcoming your hurdles (you may even choose one of the ones you identified with, but now to go deeper in that realm ... know there is always a new layer of excellence even in your strong areas).

You Are a Muse Too

Everyone has within him or her an inspiring quality, behavior, or set of beliefs. Think about what people have appreciated in or about you, particularly with what you find self-pride in. Christen these positive features about yourself as a Muse. This will deepen and strengthen your experience of yourself as the inspiring being you are. (Plus it's kind of fun.)

What would your Muse name be?

What are your powers?

Whom do you inspire?

When do "mortals" need to summon you?

What is your symbol?

What are your hobbies as this Muse?

What exercises would you have mortals do to learn more about you?

What is your motto or quote?

How would you take a walk?

What are your aspirations as a Muse?

How does this Muse make itself known in everyday life?

Depict your Muse in an art form; hang it, put it in a special book, send it to yourself.

Muse Song recommends that you do the same for a friend, parent, or mentor.

Keep Going

Keep dreaming your dream,
stay true to yourself,
choose the path of trust over fear,
revise the journey as your intuition guides you,
cultivate love of yourself and others,
know that this life as you know it now

will come to an end,
ask: "if not now, when?"
but lower the pressure,
live creatively,
let go of worry, fear, judgment
dance until the morning glories dawn their smiles,
and do at least five minutes of your creative
passion ...
every day-ish that you can.

www.ingramcontent.com/pod-product-compliance
Lightning Source LLC
Chambersburg PA
CBHW081205170426
43197CB00018B/2925